A FUNERAL MANUAL

A Funeral Manual

Perry H. Biddle, Jr.

WILLIAM B. EERDMANS PUBLISHING COMPANY
GRAND RAPIDS, MICHIGAN

First published 1976, 1984 by Abingdon Press, Nashville, Tennessee
© 1976, 1984 Abingdon Press

This updated and revised edition copyright © 1994 by
Wm. B. Eerdmans Publishing Co.
255 Jefferson Ave. S.E., Grand Rapids, Michigan 49503
All rights reserved

00 99 98 97 96 95 94   7 6 5 4 3 2 1

Library of Congress Cataloging-in-Publication Data

Biddle, Perry H., 1932-
A funeral manual / Perry H. Biddle, Jr.
p.   cm.
Rev. ed. of: Abingdon funeral manual.
Includes bibliographical references.
ISBN 0-8028-0697-X
1. Funeral service — Handbooks, manuals, etc. 2. Funeral sermons.
3. Sermons, American. I. Biddle, Perry H., 1932-
Abingdon funeral manual. II. Title.
BV199.F8B48   1994
265'.85 — dc20   94-10495
                                                          CIP

Unless otherwise noted, the Scripture quotations in this publication are from
the New Revised Standard Version of the Bible, copyright © 1989 by the
Division of Christian Education of the National Council of Churches of
Christ in the U.S.A. Used by permission.

Dedicated to the memory of my father,
Rev. P. H. Biddle,
a Presbyterian minister for 67 years,
who taught me the art of ministry

OTHER PUBLICATIONS BY THE AUTHOR

A Hospital Visitation Manual (1994)
A Marriage Manual (1994)
Abingdon Funeral Manual (1976; revised 1984)
Abingdon Marriage Manual (1974; revised 1986)
Abingdon Hospital Visitation Manual (1988)
Humor and Healing (1994)
Lectionary Preaching Workbook, Year B (1987)
Lectionary Preaching Workbook, Year C (1988)
Marrying Again (1986)
Preaching the Lectionary, Year A (1989)
Preaching the Lectionary, Year B (1990)
Preaching the Lectionary, Year C (1991)
Reflections on Suicide (1992)
The Goodness of Marriage (1984)

CONTENTS

ACKNOWLEDGMENTS

This service book seeks to furnish working pastors with a selection of funeral services and to guide them in planning and conducting the funeral service. The book also offers help in developing a funeral policy in a local church and resources for educating a congregation in death, dying, and the Christian funeral service.

I was pleased to be invited by Abingdon Press to write a replacement for the well-known *Pastor's Ideal Funeral Manual.* I am indebted to many colleagues and friends who have encouraged me in this task, a number of whom gave valuable assistance in the preparation of the earlier *Abingdon Marriage Manual.* This service book is written from a background of many years in the parish ministry and out of a deepening concern for the renewal of the Christian funeral service.

I am especially indebted to the following persons for their counsel and assistance in researching and preparing the book: the Reverend Hoyt Hickman, Board of Discipleship, The United Methodist Church; Dr. Marion J. Hatchett, School of Theology, University of the South; Dr. James C. Barry, the Sunday School Board, Southern Baptist Convention; Mrs. Bearnadean Gupton, the John A. Gupton College (School of Mortuary Science), Nashville, Tennessee; Mr. Frank Conley, Volunteer State

College; the Reverend Deryl Fleming, Ravensworth Baptist Church, Annandale, Virginia; the Reverend Beverly Asbury, Vanderbilt University; the Reverend Darrell B. Ray; Dr. T. Hartley Hall IV, Union Theological Seminary, Richmond, Virginia; Mr. Hal Hopson; the Reverend Michael W. Merriman, Associated Parishes of the Episcopal Church, Washington, D.C.; the Reverend Allen Oakley; the Reverend Ed Robertson, First Presbyterian Church, Brownsville, Texas; and the Reverend Frank Robert.

A special word of thanks is given to Dr. Harold W. Fildey (now deceased), Vanderbilt Divinity School, for reading the manuscript and offering very helpful suggestions.

Dr. John Killinger continues to inspire me in the task of writing through his warm friendship and by his own writings. I am grateful for his wise counsel and encouragement.

Finally, I wish to acknowledge and thank my wife, Sue, and my children, Lindsay and Perry III, and the members of the congregation of the First Presbyterian Church, Old Hickory, Tennessee, for their generosity in allowing me the time to prepare this service book. Without their love, interest, and support the book would not have been possible.

Old Hickory, Tennessee, 1976   PERRY H. BIDDLE, JR.

NOTE: In some of the older copyrighted material in this book, *he, him,* and *his* are used as pronouns of the common gender to include both male and female.

PREFACE TO THE REISSUE

This manual is in its third life. It was first published in 1976 as the *Abingdon Funeral Manual* and was revised in 1984. I was very pleased when Wm. B. Eerdmans Publishing Company extended a contract for reissuing the book in a revised form, since there has been a favorable response to the two earlier editions.

This completely revised book features the new Presbyterian liturgy "The Funeral: A Service of Witness to the Resurrection." There is a new sermon for the funeral of one who completed suicide, plus a section of suggested readings on suicide. The music for funerals has been revised and supplemented. The bibliography has been updated. Appropriate Scripture passages are included.

I want to thank church organists Andrew Risinger of First Presbyterian Church and Edgar Rogers of Second Presbyterian Church, Nashville, for suggesting appropriate funeral music.

A number of ministers read the former edition and made helpful suggestions. I am indebted to Rev. Donna Scott, Rev. John Collette, and Rev. John Wilkerson for their comments. Rev. Hoyt Hickman, former director of worship resources, Board of Discipleship of the United Methodist Church, was very helpful in preparing this edition and the former editions. I am also grateful to his successor, Rev. Dan Benedict, for suggestions.

I wish to thank my wife, Sue, for her encouragement and care during the past four years as I have recovered from a near-fatal car wreck. Her affirmation that "This will be a redemptive experience" is proving true, for which I am grateful to God.

This manual is written with the hope that it will help working pastors as they plan and conduct funeral services and witness to the resurrection of the body through Jesus Christ our Lord.

Nashville, Tennessee   PERRY H. BIDDLE, JR.
September 1, 1993

PREFACE TO THE REVISED EDITION

Needless to say, I have been deeply gratified by the generally favorable response to the first edition of this book designed for the working pastor. We are living in an exciting period of liturgical development, and the printing of this new edition offers an opportunity to include more recent liturgies for the burial rite and to make several other changes.

Some additional suggestions for hymns for congregational singing have been added, and some changes have been made in the bibliography.

I thank those who have assisted in this revision, especially the Reverend Hoyt Hickman of the Board of Discipleship, The United Methodist Church, whose counsel and friendship are invaluable.

1984   PERRY H. BIDDLE, JR.

PART I

ARRANGING THE FUNERAL SERVICE

1

THE CHRISTIAN FUNERAL SERVICE

The Christian funeral service is a service of worship under the direction of the minister. The purpose of the service is to worship God and comfort the mourners. The funeral service celebrates the deceased Christian's move from the church militant to the church triumphant. The funeral seeks to fill the social vacuum that results from an individual's death. It provides the proper perspective upon both death and life and offers support for the bereaved by dealing with death through the shared faith of the believing community.

An indication of the spirit in which the Christian funeral service should be conducted can be gained from the funeral practices of the early Christian church. There the funeral consisted of (1) the funeral procession from the house, (2) the singing of psalms, (3) the reading of Scripture, and (4) Communion. The distinctive mark of the Christian funeral procession was that of triumph expressed in the wearing of white, the burning of torches, the waving of palm branches, and the shouts of "Alleluia." The service was concluded at the grave with prayers.

This note of victory over death should always pervade the Christian funeral service. It should be reflected in the minister's words to and actions toward the bereaved and in the conducting of the service. The liturgical color white, symbolizing joy, is the desirable color to be worn and used in the service.

The pastor should be guided in conducting the funeral service by the heritage of the Christian faith — both Scripture and the history of the church — which emphasizes the *reality of death* and *the hope of new life.* The minister should take the lead in recapturing these fundamentals and in making use of the rich heritage of the past to create a service that is new and relevant.

An important element of the Christian heritage is the affirmation of belief in the *resurrection of the body,* in contrast to the Greek idea of the immortality of the soul. The funeral service, and especially the sermon, should hold up the biblical hope of life beyond the grave by the power of God.

Oscar Cullmann has sharply distinguished between immortality of the soul and resurrection of the dead, pointing out that immortality is only a negative assertion: The soul does not die.[1] But the biblical teaching of resurrection positively affirms that the whole person who *really died* is recalled to life by a new act of God's creation. Study of and reflection upon these two concepts in the light of the teaching of Scripture and their place in church history can enable the minister to plan and conduct the funeral service with greater meaning and effectiveness.

---

1. See Oscar Cullmann, *Immortality of the Soul or Resurrection of the Dead?* (London: Epworth Press, 1958); Krister Stendahl, ed., *Immortality and Resurrection* (New York: Macmillan, 1965); and Milton McC. Gatch, *Death: Meaning and Mortality in Christian Thought and Contemporary Culture* (New York: Seabury Press, 1969).

It is the thesis of this book that the Christian funeral can be most effective when the biblical teaching of the reality of death and the assurance of resurrection by the power of God are kept in dynamic tension. Facing the reality of death enables the Christian to grieve, but not as one who has no hope. The assurance of resurrection from the dead gives a sustaining hope to those who grieve. The funeral service, especially the sermon, should affirm the biblical approach.

Changes are taking place in the liturgies of the church, especially in the liturgy of the burial service. There is a move away from the mood of the dread of death as a judgment on sin to a joyous, triumphant note of hope based on the resurrection of Jesus Christ. The difference between these two attitudes in the Christian context is as great as that between black and white, the colors used in the funeral service by the early pagans and Christians, respectively.

Perhaps the reality of death and the hope of new life are best expressed in the New Orleans jazz funeral. On the way to the cemetery the funeral procession is accompanied by slow, somber dirges. But returning from the burial, the musicians burst forth into joyful affirmations of life! Does this not say something of significance to those who conduct and participate in the funeral service?

In leading the funeral service and ministering to the bereaved, the roles of pastor and preacher merge as nowhere else in the pastoral ministry. The minister, in leading the service, and especially in the funeral message, looks out on faces hungry for a word from on high, searching for a message of assurance and hope in the face of the mystery of death. The funeral service may provide an opportunity for the minister to be of help later to those who grieve, as well as bringing the comforting Word of God. Grief can open a window to the soul.

The chapters that follow attempt to provide guidance and resources for the minister who confronts the very difficult task of planning and conducting the Christian funeral service. By the grace of God, the minister can witness to the resurrection of Jesus Christ in both word and action by conducting the burial service in the Christian context and, by so doing, enable all those who participate to know that

> "Death is swallowed up in victory."
> "O death, where is thy victory?
> O death, where is thy sting?"

The sting of death is sin, and the power of sin is the law. But thanks be to God, who gives us the victory through our Lord Jesus Christ.

(1 Cor. 15:54b-57, RSV)

2

PLANNING THE SERVICE

The minister is in charge of the funeral or memorial worship service.[1] Whether acting alone or in conjunction with others, as the leader of the worshiping community the minister will take an active role in planning the service.

The pastor is sometimes with the family when one of its members dies. Or the pastor may be notified by a member or friend of the family or by the funeral director. If not present at the time of death, the minister will want to make a pastoral call as soon as possible. The time and place of the funeral service will be determined by the family with the concurrence of the pastor and funeral director.

Occasionally a funeral director will determine the time of a funeral service before consulting the pastor. Whether done from oversight or pressure of scheduling funerals, this can place the minister in a difficult position if there is a conflicting engagement such as another funeral or a wedding. Future occurrences may be avoided by tactfully discussing with the funeral director the problem this has created and asking that in the

---

1. *Funeral service* will be used to denote the worship service for the burial of the dead, whether the body is present or not, unless otherwise indicated.

future notification be made earlier. If several ministers in a community discover that they share this problem, they may wish to arrange a conference with the manager of the funeral establishment to request consultation before setting the time of funerals. Most funeral directors are cooperative in this matter.

The pastor may be assisted in planning the funeral service by one or more members of the family or friends of the deceased. These persons may have specific requests regarding the content of the service and the way in which it will be conducted. Or they may offer only general suggestions, leaving the details to the discretion of the pastor. In many instances, the minister alone plans the service. It may be for a parishioner the pastor knows well, in which case the task is much easier. Or it may be for a stranger about whom the pastor knows very little. In every instance, thoughtful, careful planning can make the difference between a creative worship service that boldly witnesses to the resurrection and offers comfort to the bereaved, and one that does not.

For many people brevity is the chief criterion of a successful funeral service. In a number of instances, families request that the service be brief, in protest against the excessively long and maudlin services of the past. But whether brief or of moderate length, the funeral that is well planned will be more effective in achieving the goal of worshiping God and comforting the mourners.

The funeral service is distinguished from the memorial service chiefly by the relationship of the body of the deceased to the worship service. In a funeral service the body either is present or is an integral part of the funeral process. But the body is neither present during nor a part of the memorial service. The word *funeral* comes from a Sanskrit word meaning *smoke* and refers to the cremation rites used in the disposition of a body. The worship service may properly be called a funeral service if the body is laid to rest immediately prior to or after the service, even if it is not present in the service. A memorial service or services may be held at the same time as the funeral service, or at other times, or at other places, or on the anniversary of a death.

The funeral and the memorial service may be planned in much the same fashion. The memorial service will have less emphasis on the body of the deceased, and for this reason it may more easily focus on the worship of God and the Christian's victory over death. It may or may not be less emotional than the funeral service.

In some parts of the country the committal service is attended only by the immediate family and close friends. A funeral service follows at the church. Many pastors who follow this practice report that it is more helpful to the bereaved than the funeral service followed by the committal. While there may be some value in having the body present during the funeral worship service, the coffin should remain closed during and after the service.

In the remainder of this chapter, the planning of the funeral service under various circumstances will be presented. Planning with the family and friends of the deceased, planning with the terminally ill patient, planning in advance, and planning the funeral alone will be discussed.

PLANNING WITH THE FAMILY

The majority of funeral services are planned by the pastor in conjunction with family and close friends of the deceased. In some instances, work associates, teachers, and others who knew the deceased may be invited to share in the planning. The minister listens to and leads those who plan the service, making certain that the service is one of Christian worship and expressive of the feelings of the bereaved.

The pastor, upon making the initial visit to the bereaved, offers assistance. The family may ask that another cleric be invited to join in the service. In such cases the pastor extends the invitation on behalf of the family. It is accepted ministerial etiquette that the pastor of the deceased leads in conducting the service, with other clergy assisting. After the pastor is asked to conduct the service, a convenient time is arranged to meet with family and friends for planning. A quiet place apart from the flow of visitors is desirable.

The pastor should arrive at the planning interview with a copy of a funeral service book, note pad, and other materials such as a hymnal and sample copies of funeral services. The pastor may suggest an outline for the funeral service, if the church has no prescribed liturgy. Keeping in mind that Christian worship involves the proclamation of the gospel and the congregation's response to it, the pastor may suggest an order of service similar to the following, which may be adapted or abbreviated as the occasion demands:

Call to Worship (scriptural)
Hymn (by congregation)
Prayer of Invocation
Old Testament Lessons
Gloria Patri, Hymn, or Special Music

New Testament Lessons
Affirmation of Faith (Apostles' Creed or other)
Hymn (by congregation)
Sermon
Pastoral Prayer
Benediction

If the church has a written guideline on funerals, the pastor may wish to review this with the family.[2] Since the family seldom will have worked out details for the funeral service at this time, the pastor has the opportunity to suggest ways for the service to witness to the resurrection and comfort the bereaved.

The minister may ask if there are specific requests regarding Scripture to be read and hymns to be sung. *Choice heightens awareness.* The process of making selections can enable family members to become more aware of the purpose of the Christian funeral service. The act of selecting is something positive the bereaved can do when they feel so helpless in the shock of grief. And the family members will respond more readily to those parts of the service that they have helped to choose. Gentle but firm guidance on the part of the minister can enable wise planning of the funeral service.

The nature of the funeral sermon may be discussed at this time.[3] Some families request that there be no eulogy. The funeral message may or may not include a specific reference to the deceased by name. However, there should

2. See Chapter 6, "Developing a Church Policy on Funerals," and the bibliography.
3. See Chapter 5, "The Funeral Sermon."

be a place in the service — in the sermon, prayer, or else-where — to acknowledge and give thanks for the life of the deceased by name. The message should be brief, usually between seven and ten minutes in length. Prayers are usually left entirely to the discretion of the pastor. When the service is informal, members of the congregation may offer prayers of thanksgiving for some facet of the deceased person's life. The prayers in the funeral service are often the most effective means for comforting the bereaved.

The committal service — at the grave, crematorium, mausoleum, or at sea — is brief and adapted to the particular situation. It usually consists of words of Scripture, the committal prayer, and benediction. A creed of the church may be affirmed, and the doxology or other hymn may be sung.

In some instances the entire funeral service is conducted where the remains are to be laid to rest. This service combines an abbreviated funeral service and committal service. Graveside services only are often held for the interment of an infant or for an adult when there are few people to attend the service.

Procedures at the committal vary in different areas of the country and among denominations. Some traditions prescribe the lowering of the coffin to its final resting place before the committal begins. This can be a symbolic act pointing to the finality of death. The casting of three handfuls of earth onto the coffin is a part of the liturgy of some churches. While some clergy omit the phrase "ashes to ashes, dust to dust," these words can help emphasize the reality and finality of death. Family, clergy, and friends may help to cover the grave.

These procedures and options may be discussed when planning the service.

Planning in Advance of Need

When asked by a parishioner to assist in planning a funeral service in advance of need, the pastor has a unique opportunity to help clarify the person's desires and to offer informed counsel regarding the Christian funeral service. A form for use in planning the service can be helpful. It should include space to indicate the person's requests for hymns, Scripture, music, sermon, place of service, and clergy. In addition, the form may indicate the individual's wishes regarding the donation of body organs, body disposition, and so on. One copy should be filed in the church office, another copy should be kept by the individual, and a third copy should be given to a relative or close friend.

One Lutheran congregation engaged in a study of death and funeral practices, during which the pastor and resource persons from the community led sessions on the medical, legal, religious, and social aspects of death and the funeral. As a result, the pastor had a number of requests for assistance in planning services.

Such planning allows the minister to deal at length with requests for inappropriate music, poetry, or other items. The role of fraternal and military organizations in the service can be discussed. A church policy prepared and adopted by the governing body of the congregation can be helpful in guiding persons who plan their own service.[4]

4. See Chapter 6, "Developing a Church Policy on Funerals."

Planning with the Terminally Ill Patient

The initiative should always lie with the patient in discussing his or her own funeral service. The point at which the patient may wish to discuss the funeral will vary from person to person. Or it may not be expressed at all. This, too, should be respected as the individual's right to privacy.

However, when patients do raise the subject of planning their own services, pastors should be open and supportive. A warm, honest, and accepting atmosphere will enable patients to express more easily their feelings regarding death and their wishes for the funeral service.

Planning the funeral service will cause some individuals to reflect upon the meaning of their lives and how best to celebrate that meaning. It can be a means of expressing their hope in Christ and the affirmation of life beyond the grave. Planning their own funerals may enable patients to accept death more fully.

Perhaps the best assistance that can be given to the terminally ill patient is the pastor's own attitude toward death and empathy with the person. The intensity of emotions involved in openly facing one's imminent death with another may bring forth deeper feelings and values than are aroused in any other circumstances. The pastor can enable the patient to shape the service to express these deep feelings about life and death.

Planning Alone

In some instances the full responsibility for planning a funeral service will fall on the minister's shoulders, with no assistance from others. The pastor will want to seek as much information as can be gained about the deceased in order to make the service as meaningful as possible. Members of the family, friends, and associates may share with the pastor information about the deceased. The minister will keep in mind the various aspects of the particular funeral: the life and the conditions of death of the deceased; the needs of the bereaved; and the physical setting for the service, including the anticipated attendance of friends and family.

There should be unity and movement in the funeral worship service. All of the music and readings should contribute to the theme of the Christian funeral as a witness to the resurrection.

Planning the funeral service can be a meaningful experience for all involved. It calls forth the best liturgical skills and creative talents of the pastor. It can be therapeutic for persons planning their own funeral service or that of a loved one.

3

CONDUCTING THE SERVICE

General Guidelines

The pastor is in charge of the funeral worship service and works in close cooperation with the funeral director. It is desirable that the family notify the pastor *before* notifying the funeral director if at all possible, so that the pastor can counsel them regarding arrangements. When desired, the pastor may contact the funeral director for the family.

It cannot be stressed too strongly that the minister should make certain that the time and place of the funeral service and interment are recorded on the calendar of the church and on the minister's own calendar.[1] Every precaution should be taken to ensure that the minister does not forget a commitment to conduct a funeral service or arrive at the wrong time or place. Sufficient time must be allowed to get to the funeral service, and possible delays due to traffic and weather conditions should be anticipated. If the service is not held at the pastor's own church, the funeral director should be contacted immediately upon arriving at the place of the funeral.

When preparing to conduct the funeral service it is

---

1. *Interment* will be used in referring to the disposition of the body by whatever means, unless otherwise indicated.

helpful to write down the order of service to be followed and to prepare copies for the funeral director and the musicians. A worship service bulletin, when used, will serve this purpose and enable the participants to carry out their roles without mishap.

Funeral practices vary across ethnic, denominational, and regional lines. There are so many variations that it is beyond the scope of this book to deal with each one. However, there are general guidelines to follow, which may be varied according to the particular situation. A pastor new to an area would do well to learn from members of the church's worship commission, or from other clergy, the practices unique to the area.

Prior to the actual funeral service, the pastor will have occasion to be with the family, either at home, at the funeral chapel, at the church, or wherever the body is placed and the family gathers to receive friends. Although the traditional wake is held less frequently now, the family members and friends usually gather in the evening(s) prior to the funeral to console one another. On these occasions, the pastor may lead a brief service of Scripture and prayer and give words of comfort. It may also be a time for sharing memories and reflecting on the meaning of the loved one's life.

The final closing of the coffin immediately before the funeral service can be especially traumatic for the bereaved. Family solidarity in the face of death can be affirmed through the joining of hands for prayer led by the pastor. It is strongly recommended that the closing of the coffin take place *before* the funeral itself begins. Many ministers and some funeral directors strongly believe that the coffin should *remain closed* during and after the funeral service.

Often family members do not know what to do in this regard. The funeral director waits for their request or may suggest that the coffin be left open or reopened. The pastor should discuss this with the family ahead of time. It might be pointed out that closing the coffin will enable everyone to focus more easily upon God and his mercy during the service. Much of what the funeral service seeks to do may be undone by viewing the body again at the end of the service.

However, this practice can be difficult to change. Pastors may encounter resistance from both funeral directors and local custom. After developing a level of trust with their congregations, pastors may be able to lead them to accept the closing of coffins before services begin.

Whether or not there is a funeral procession will depend upon the church's liturgy, the location of the service, and the desires of the family and the minister. When the service is conducted in a funeral home, a chapel, or at the home of the deceased, there may be no procession. Often the coffin is already in the chapel in position for the service. When there is a procession, the minister leads, followed by the pallbearers, the coffin, and the family. If acolytes are used, they precede the minister.

The congregation stands when the procession enters and remains standing until the family is seated. Standing may be led by members of the congregation familiar with this custom or by a signal from the minister. Upon entering the church or chapel, the minister may speak words from Scripture such as "I am the resurrection and the life; he who believes in me, though he die, yet shall he live, and whoever lives and believes in me shall never die" (John 11:25-26, RSV). When the coffin is in position and the family is seated in the front pews, the minister will indicate that the congregation is to be seated.

When two or more ministers share in leading the service, portions are either assigned by the pastor of the deceased at the request of the family or are mutually agreed upon by the participating clergy. An order of service for each minister is desirable.

When the celebration of the Lord's Supper is requested by the family and is permitted by the church's tradition, the minister makes arrangements for the sacrament with the proper persons. The Lord's Supper may be celebrated as the climax of the funeral service or, when church policy permits, in the home of the family at the conclusion of a shared meal.

The celebration of the Lord's Supper at a funeral has good theological and historical foundations. In some Protestant churches it is not observed in connection with a funeral. However, in many churches this ancient practice may become a meaningful part of the funeral service again. It can help those who participate in it to focus on Christ's victory over death and his abiding presence with believers.

At the conclusion of the service the minister gestures for the congregation to rise for the benediction and the recessional. In some churches the benediction used at the funeral service is the one that is most commonly associated with Holy Communion. This serves, by association, as a reminder of the victory of the risen Christ over death.

After the benediction, the minister leads the procession from the church, followed by the coffin and the family. Pallbearers either carry the coffin or, when a carriage is used to move it, precede the coffin. The minister stands near the door of the hearse, facing it as the coffin is placed inside, then departs for the trip to the grave.

The committal service is held either before or after the funeral service. In inclement weather the minister should consider the health of the family and friends and should shape the service to be as meaningful and brief as possible. The ceremony at the grave is the turning point of the entire funeral service. The bereaved must release the dead.

When the family members have been seated or are standing in their places at the graveside, the minister begins the committal. The funeral director may give the cue when the coffin is positioned. It is becoming more common to lower the coffin into its final resting place at this point.

The solidarity of the bereaved and the community at the time of death is extremely important. When the funeral is conducted in the church, the family members are seated in the front center pews. In a funeral chapel, too, they should be seated in these pews, rather than in a "family area" screened from the view of the congregation.

Although the conducting of the funeral service ends at the grave, the family will find it very helpful if a pastoral call is made later the same day. During this time the bereaved begin to put together the meaning of the entire death experience. Often they share a common meal and, in so doing, act out their unity and hope for the lives they will go on living. This is an opportunity for the minister to join the bereaved in affirming life. This pastoral ministry should continue as long as needed. Help in shaping this ministry can be found in the bibliography.

A Service for a Stillborn Infant

The minister will want to talk with the parents of the stillborn infant in order to determine the nature of the service. If they consider the stillborn child as having been a person who died, then a funeral service for a child is in order. The Presbyterian funeral liturgy has guidance for such a child's funeral.

In the case of a miscarriage, a healing service for the bereaved is appropriate. This would involve as many family members and friends who wish to gather for a brief service.[2] The healing would focus on the grief of the shattered hopes of parents, family, and friends.

The funeral service for a stillborn infant is usually a graveside service and is designed for the particular occasion.

The service might consist of Scripture, remarks, and prayer, concluding with the benediction. The Apostles' Creed and Lord's Prayer might also be used. Some Scripture passages appropriate for the occasion are Job 14; Psalm 39; and Hosea 11:1-4, 8-9. The remarks should emphasize the comfort of God, the assurance that nothing can separate us from the love of God, and the resurrection hope.

2. See the service of anointing in my book *A Hospital Visitation Manual* (Grand Rapids: William B. Eerdmans, 1994).

4

MUSIC AND OTHER RESOURCES

Music

Music for the funeral service should be selected on the basis of its appropriateness for Christian worship. Two of the chief faults of the music sometimes used are found in the theology of the words and in the music itself. The words should express a biblical understanding of God's mercy and power and the meaning of life and death. The music for the funeral need not be funereal in tone![1]

Of all types of music available for the funeral service, congregational hymns are the most fitting and meaningful. Hymns familiar to the bereaved take on an added dimension when sung or played for the funeral. When selecting hymns, one may ask whether these hymns witness to the resurrection of Jesus Christ, convey the strong comfort of God, and hold up the Christian's hope of resurrection. Two hymns that, though often used in funerals, fail to meet these criteria of good funeral music are "Beautiful Isle of Somewhere" and "I Come to the Garden Alone."

Music in the funeral service may reflect many moods. It may express sorrow and joy, but the dominant note

1. See Appendix 1, pp. 173-77 below, for suggested music.

should be that of the victory over death found in Easter hymns. It may be meditative, or it may be vigorous and triumphant in tone. Maudlin and sentimental music should be discouraged. However, music that appeals to the emotions and music that expresses objective truth are fitting. The once common notion that music in a minor key is always sad is refuted by the majestic triumph of much of the music by Bach and other composers.

There is a movement away from employing soloists and small groups of vocalists in the funeral service. Rather, congregational singing led by a choir, when available, is becoming more common. This is commendable. When the funeral service is conducted from a funeral chapel or other place where hymnals are not available, the words of the hymns may be included in a bulletin.

The wise minister will honor requests from the family for particular music whenever possible. The occasion of a funeral is not the time to attempt a program of music education. However, over a period of time the quality of music used in a church's funeral services can be improved through the influence of the pastor and church musicians. But requests for favorite hymns of the deceased or the bereaved should be given high priority in planning the service, since the music may be of special comfort and meaning.

Seldom are instruments other than the piano or organ used in traditional funeral services. However, in contemporary and experimental-style funeral services, the guitar, flute, and other instruments are being used. A chamber music group is also appropriate.

Music piped into a funeral chapel should not be played as background music during the service. When only taped music is available, the minister should make appropriate selections and indicate when they are to be played.

POETRY

It is not within the scope of this manual to list the many poems appropriate for use in the funeral service. Poetry from a variety of sources — Dag Hammarskjöld, Edna St. Vincent Millay, John Donne — may be chosen and effectively employed in the service. Collections of religious verse may be consulted for appropriate selections. The theology of each poem should be carefully evaluated for its Christian thrust and contribution to the total worship service.

LITANIES

Those who prepare the funeral service may wish to include a personalized litany. A member of the family or a friend of the deceased may compose and read such a litany. If a bulletin containing the litany is not used, the response of the people may be announced at the beginning: "We praise you, O Lord" or "Comfort those who sorrow, O God." The first part of the litany may center on God's attributes of power, love, steadfast mercy, and so forth, and the second part may highlight the life and contributions of the deceased, with thanks given in the response: "We thank you, O God."

Litanies found in a hymnal or worship book may also be used. Litanies not only involve the congregation more actively in the funeral service but also encourage the dialogue with God that should characterize the funeral service as a whole.

Prayers

Some funeral liturgies contain prayers, while others leave the composing of the prayers entirely to the minister. When there is freedom to compose prayers, it is helpful to reflect upon these before conducting the service. Scripture, hymns, and prayers from the rich heritage of the church can provide ideas and phrases for inclusion.

While some may prefer to write out prayers in full, others are more comfortable with a list of items and persons. This list enables the minister to include all those needs and persons without the danger of forgetting some, yet allows greater freedom and spontaneity than prayers that are written out in full.

The following prayer or a similar one may be used at the beginning of the funeral service:

> Almighty God, our heavenly Father, who loves us with an everlasting love, and can turn the darkness of sorrow into the morning, help us to be open to you in this hour. Give us reverent and submissive hearts. Speak to us of eternal things by your Spirit through Scripture and the experience of worship. Give us hope, O Lord, that we may be able to pass safely through the valley of the shadow of death into the light of your presence. Grant us peace, through Christ we pray. *Amen.*[2]

A prayer that may be used as the pastoral prayer after the readings from the Scriptures is as follows:

2. Adapted from *The Book of Common Order* of the Church of Scotland (Oxford: Oxford University Press, 1940).

Gracious God, who has sent your Son into the world to bring eternal life, we thank you that by his death he conquered death. We thank you that by your power he was raised from the dead as the firstfruits of those who have died. May we know the assurance that because he lives we shall live also and that neither death nor life, things present nor things to come, shall be able to separate us from your steadfast love.

God of comfort, who comforts us as one who is comforted by his mother, uphold your sorrowing people with your everlasting arms. Enable them to find in you their refuge and strength and to know the love of Christ which passes knowledge. Give to them faith and love and hope in Christ our crucified and risen Lord who has opened the gates of everlasting life.

We thank you for all your servants who have died in the faith. We give special thanks for him (her) whom you have called home. We remember your goodness and mercy to him (her) during this earthly life, and we thank you. We give thanks that for him (her) all sickness and sorrow are over and that death itself is overcome.

We pray for ourselves, O God, asking that we may be given the faith and strength to live out our lives faithful to you. When our earthly lives are ended may we be gathered with those we love in the kingdom of your glory, where there will be no more death, sorrow, crying, or pain. For these things of life will have passed away. Through Jesus Christ our Lord. *Amen*.[3]

3. Adapted from *The Book of Common Order.*

At the committal service a prayer may be offered, after which the benediction is given. This prayer is usually brief and may be as follows:

> O God, our help in ages past, our hope for years to come, be near to us and comfort us. We thank you that Jesus Christ has destroyed death and by his rest in the tomb has sanctified the graves of the faithful. We thank you for that victory over death and the grave which he has given us and all those who die in him. Raise us up from the death of sin to the life of righteousness, so that when we die we may rest in Christ. When we die may we receive the blessing, "Well done, good and faithful servant, enter into the joy of your Lord." Through Christ our risen Lord we pray. *Amen.*

The purpose of this chapter is not only to suggest aids for worship in the funeral service but also to serve as an impetus to the pastor to seek out other materials and to create additional resources. A file of such resources can prove invaluable when the pastor is suddenly called upon to plan a funeral service. A few books of appropriate resources, copies of collected services, and an inspired imagination can be most welcome.

5

THE FUNERAL SERMON

The funeral sermon is a unique proclamation of the gospel, in that each sermon should be a special creation for a particular person, the deceased. Ideally it will reflect the minister's own knowledge of the deceased and understanding of the needs of the bereaved. If the pastor does not know the one who has died, the sermon could seem either impersonal or falsely personal. However, by talking to members of the family and associates of the deceased, the pastor may gather information to assist in creating an appropriate sermon. The aim of this chapter is to guide the minister in the task of developing the funeral sermon through a description of the message and the various approaches that may be used in constructing it.

Two Foci

John Killinger has said that "the geometrical description of preaching is an ellipse, not a circle, with two foci, not one: God *and* persons. Our preaching is for people. It is from God (that is our high hope), but it is for people."[1] The funeral sermon, perhaps more than any other, should

1. Killinger, *The Centrality of Preaching* (Waco, Tex.: Word Books, 1969), p. 60.

keep these two foci in proper perspective. In preparing the sermon, the minister seeks to discover what God is saying to this particular group of people in the face of death. To do this, the nature of the death must be kept in mind — whether it was sudden or after a long illness; the age, sex, and vocation of the deceased; and the relationship between the deceased and the bereaved. The minister should also be aware of the contribution of the one who has died to the community and his or her vocational achievements. In addition, the pastor will want to be sensitive to the particular needs of the bereaved, insofar as they can be determined.

Purpose

Since the purpose of the Christian funeral is to worship God and to comfort the mourners, the funeral sermon should be developed with this overarching purpose in mind. It should point the congregation to the Triune God who has created us, redeemed us, and who sustains and comforts us. The majesty, power, steadfast love, and wisdom of God should be lifted up and celebrated in the sermon. Because the ultimate comfort of the bereaved is to be found in God's mercy, a funeral message that points the bereaved to God will be of greater comfort than one that focuses only on the feelings of the bereaved.

Related to the Living

The funeral message should enable those present to reflect upon their own living and dying in light of the gospel. It may point out that the act of dying is only a dramatic symbol of what has been happening all along, the passage through death to life. Each Christian dies little deaths to old habits and experiences little resurrections to new ways of being. Such a faith accepts the fact of the resurrection as the central fact of the Christian gospel. It affirms that the One who died on Golgotha was indeed the pioneer, the first to experience death's full reality. In him death is swallowed up. Victory is won!

VARIETY OF APPROACHES

The funeral message should develop a single truth and should either be based on a biblical passage or express a biblical point of view of life and death. The following are some of the approaches that may be taken.

Biographical. The biographical sermon is based on the life of a biblical character such as David, whose little son died, and illustrates that faith sustained him in sorrow (2 Sam. 12:19-23). This passage, especially fitting for the funeral of an infant or child, shows how David accepted the child's death: "I shall go to him, but he will not return to me" (2 Sam. 12:23).

Doctrinal. Although each funeral message should point to the resurrection, the doctrinal sermon develops a particular theological concept. There is a widespread and persistent interest in the future life. The funeral message that takes this interest into account will find a receptive hearing. A sermon on the providence of God, encompassing the mystery of suffering and tragedy, is especially appropriate for a funeral.

Expository. Based on an exegesis of a biblical passage, this sermon declares God's word to a particular people and their needs. Passages from Paul's letters in which he discusses resurrection are especially appropriate.

Life Situation. This approach begins with the congregation as it mourns a particular death and moves on to express God's comforting love. This is one of the most effective methods for developing the funeral message.

Occasional. The occasional sermon is developed around the death or the funeral. If the death occurred after a long illness or as a suicide or murder, the sermon may focus on this fact. Or if it occurred on Christmas, Easter, or some other special occasion, the sermon may take this into account. Or the death or funeral may be directly related to some occasion in the deceased's life such as a birthday or wedding anniversary.

Textual. The textual sermon is constructed on a single verse or part of a verse of Scripture relevant to the funeral occasion. Appropriate texts may be found with the use of a concordance, and a selected number are given later in this chapter. The pastor, in his or her general study of the Bible, may note texts that seem to be especially suitable for use later in a funeral message.

COMMEMORATION

The funeral sermon may or may not include a eulogy. If it does not, it is appropriate to recognize and give thanks by name for the life of the deceased elsewhere in the service. In commemorating the life of the one who has died, the sermon may include humorous and tragic moments in the person's life, surveying the frustrations, limitations, and successes. This is quite different from the traditional eulogy, which only speaks well of the deceased, often in flattering terms. While not shying away from feelings, commemoration does not elicit emotion for its own sake. Rather, it seeks to re-create the world of which the deceased was a part and thus affirm both the life and the death of the person. Such recognition assists the mourners in recalling memories of the one who has died, which is a part of the mourning process whereby God enables us to build a new future. Commemoration reassures those present that life has meaning.

More informal funeral services, especially the experimental form of worship service, may give opportunity for those present to share in creating the funeral message by relating events and experiences associated with the deceased. The minister may sum up these shared memories and relate the gospel to them.

Some ministers make it a practice never to mention the deceased in the funeral sermon, either because they did not know the person or because the difficulty of being publicly honest is too great. In some communities a eulogy is expected. The pastor would do well to reserve some freedom as to how the life of the deceased should be commemorated.

THE MOURNING PROCESS

One of the most helpful things about the funeral message is that it may address the mourning process the bereaved are just beginning. The sermon should deal honestly with the reality of the death, pointing out that the grief wound cannot heal fully until one has accepted the reality of the loss.[2] It

2. See Granger E. Westberg, *Good Grief* (Philadelphia: Fortress Press, 1962).

should encourage the bereaved, with God's grace, to surrender to some degree their emotional ties to and investment in the deceased. Pointing to the future, the sermon will encourage the mourners to form other relationships to provide new sources of emotional strength.

In the funeral service the minister uses familiar rituals, Scripture, and Christian teaching to renew the mourners' experience of basic trust. The challenge to the minister is to make these meaningful and "living" symbols, especially through the funeral sermon, so that they strengthen the trustful quality of relationships the mourners have with God and the community of believers.

RELATIONAL THEOLOGY

Proclaiming the gospel relationally can be one of the most helpful ways to create a more meaningful funeral message. God's love for the deceased and the loved one's response to this love in a life of faithful service may be celebrated. God's comforting mercy through other persons and their supportive love can help the mourners bear their grief more easily. The sermon may deal with the transition from a living relationship to that of a relationship through memory. The good news of God's grace to free, heal, and renew relationships will make the funeral message a greater source of comfort.

FACING NEGATIVE FEELINGS

The funeral message should deal with feelings — negative as well as positive. It should not seek to avoid the reality of the death by referring to it as "passing on" or "passing away." The minister should be sensitive to feelings the mourners may have of anger toward God, fear of the future, loneliness, and even despair. By facing the reality of death and the negative feelings that death evokes, the funeral message may enable the bereaved to hear the good news more clearly and respond more easily in healthy grieving.

Use of Multimedia

Funeral proclamations, especially in experimental worship services, are using multimedia and the fine arts in the task of interpreting the meaning of life and death and the good news in Jesus Christ. Slides, videos, and movies made by the deceased may be shown. An interpretive dance of one of the psalms may be performed. Readings from literature that was a favorite of the deceased or that sums up a facet of the person's life may be read by the minister or by others.

Banners, art, and original music may also be used in creating the funeral sermon. John Killinger shows how worship may be structured to evoke the fullest response from the participants, and his insights may be used in the sermon.[3] With the shift in emphasis in the Christian funeral service from gloom, symbolized by black, to joyful affirmation, symbolized by white, the sermon also may take on new forms more in keeping with its content.

---

3. See Killinger, *The Centrality of Preaching.*

SERMON SUBJECTS AND TEXTS

The following texts and subjects are provided to help the minister in building appropriate funeral sermons for various occasions.

For a Child

1 Sam. 1:28	The dedication of a child to God
2 Sam. 12:23	Hope for reunion with a child
Isa. 40:11	The shepherd gathers the lambs
Matt. 18:2-14	Jesus and little children
Matt. 19:14	Jesus welcomes children

For a Young Person

Job 1:21	A father grieves for his children
Eccles. 12:1	A youth's religion
Luke 7:14	Jesus raises a young man
1 John 2:14	The strength of youth

For One in the Middle Years

Job 19:25	My redeemer lives!
Matt. 11:28-30	Jesus' gracious invitation
John 11:25-26	I am the resurrection and the life
John 14:27	The peace of the Master
1 Cor. 15:57	The Christian's victory

For an Older Person

Gen. 15:15	Peace at the end of many years

| Ps. 91:16 | The glory of a long life |
| 2 Tim. 4:7-8 | I have kept the faith |

For One Who Has Suffered

Deut. 33:27	The everlasting arms
Job 1:21	Blessed be the name of the Lord
Rom. 5:3-5	The fruits of suffering
Rom. 8:18	Present suffering and future glory
Rom. 8:28	Confidence in God's working

For a Christian Father

| Gen. 18:19 | A godly father's teaching |
| 1 Kings 2:2-3 | A father's charge to his son |

For a Christian Mother

Prov. 31:10-31	A woman who fears the Lord
Isa. 66:13	As one whom his mother comforts
2 Tim. 1:5	The influence of a godly mother

For Other Persons

Mal. 2:5-7	The pastor of a church
Matt. 25:21	A faithful servant of God
Rom 8:38-39	A suicide
1 Tim. 3:1-7	A church leader
1 Tim. 3:13	A deacon

See Appendix 2 for model sermons.

6

DEVELOPING A CHURCH POLICY
ON FUNERALS

Local congregations and church judicatories are becoming more aware of their responsibility to persons at the time of death. The pastor working alone may have little success in changing funeral customs that are less than Christian, but she or he does have a unique opportunity to lead others in reevaluating the funeral service and funeral customs within a community. Rituals are tightly patterned and express a certain worldview. This is particularly true of the funeral ritual. But the very heart of the gospel is that change is possible in both individuals and institutions.

Joseph E. McCabe tells how he and a congregation he served went about changing the funeral practices of a local church.[1] Whereas four out of five funerals were held outside the church in the three years before the special study and program of change were begun, four out of five in the next year were held in the church.

McCabe began by sharing his concern about un-Christian and unhelpful funeral practices with members of his official board, funeral directors, and people in the parish

1. *The Power of God in a Parish Program* (Philadelphia: Westminster Press, 1959), pp. 73ff.

itself. When interest was sufficiently aroused, he preached a sermon on the Christian funeral. The sermon was printed and circulated with a covering letter commending it to the members for careful study. Later it was printed in a widely read religious journal.

The problem lies with the church, says McCabe, and nothing is going to change unless the church takes a strong lead. Some of the issues dealt with in the sermon were the place where the service is held, selection of music, the closing of the coffin before the service, the role of fraternal organizations, and the funeral sermon.

A similar strategy can be followed in other churches. While unable to effect major changes alone, the pastor can raise the level of consciousness of persons regarding the funeral and lead others who share a common concern to bring about needed changes. The commission on worship of a local church or church judicatory may study funeral practices and make recommendations to the governing body for adoption. When adopted, such a funeral guideline should be publicized among the members of the church.

A funeral statement paper can be a valuable aid to the pastor in helping persons plan funerals. It can stimulate individuals to reflect on the purpose of the Christian funeral and to make arrangements that will express a Christian view of death. Such a policy paper when given to funeral directors can prevent misunderstandings and conflict between ministers and funeral directors and enable the directors to do their job efficiently.

One of the most common complaints of the clergy regarding funeral directors is their tendency, on occasion, to usurp ecclesiastical prerogatives. Conflict sometimes occurs because of poor communication. A written policy statement regarding funeral services can help prevent this and will promote greater cooperation among all those involved. A copy given to the florist regarding the flower arrangements allowed in the church for a funeral will be helpful.

Depending upon the form of church government and the will of the governing body adopting the policy statement, it may be either a guideline or a list of specific rules, or maybe a combination of the two. Some of the areas that an effective funeral policy may cover are the following.

PLACE OF SERVICE

Among many clergy and some Christian funeral directors, there is a strong conviction that the Christian funeral service should be conducted in the church rather than in the funeral chapel. The church is the place into which one is carried as an infant. One is baptized there, unites with the people of God there, is married there, and is nourished there in the Christian faith. Thus it is fitting that the last rites for the Christian be conducted in the church.

In some instances the funeral will be conducted from the family home or at the graveside. But the great majority of funerals in many areas are held in the funeral chapel, and the clergy must be prepared to conduct it there.

CONTACTING THE MINISTER

It is preferable that the minister be contacted *first* when a death has occurred and then for the minister to consult the funeral director. *A family should feel free to consult the pastor regarding funeral expenses.* This is a touchy subject for funeral directors. Those in the funeral business often argue that people do not ask their minister's advice in picking out a car, home, or other major item. Therefore, the argument goes, the pastor should keep his or her hands off when the family faces decisions regarding funeral costs.

But decisions regarding funeral expenses are unique. The death often occurs unexpectedly and the family has not investigated funeral costs. The grief-stricken family is at a disadvantage. The minister is trained to understand grief, and to support and counsel those in grief, and may offer to accompany the bereaved to the coffin showroom when it is sensed that counsel may be needed and appreciated.

TIME OF SERVICE

It is usually desirable to avoid having funerals on Sundays or on special days of the church year such as Christmas and Good Friday. The minister should be consulted before the time of the funeral service is set so that the date may be cleared on his or her schedule.

DISPOSITION OF THE REMAINS

The congregation's position on the willing of one's organs to the living and one's body to medical science may be stated. Some persons have questions regarding cremation. While cremation has been rejected in the past by some because it "destroyed" the remains, someone has pointed out that Christian martyrs who were burned at the stake will surely be resurrected and therefore cremation is acceptable! Entombment in a mausoleum is also becoming more common.

Repose of the Body

The body is usually placed at either the funeral home or the family home before the funeral service, but it also may be placed in the church or a public building. Friends may come to any of these places for prayer and to comfort the family in their grief.

Opening and Closing of the Coffin

The value of viewing the body is open to debate. If the fundamental issue is the reality of death, then viewing the body prior to the funeral and having it present at the service may have a positive effect. On the other hand, some see no positive value in viewing the body. They feel that hanging onto the dead physical remains does not aid the bereaved in facing the future. Rather, it hinders a deeper acceptance of the present fact and a determination to make the most of the future.

It is the opinion of this writer that the coffin should be closed before the funeral begins and should remain closed afterward. A policy statement by the church will be of help to both the family and the funeral director in dealing with the closing of the coffin.

Music

The music selected for use at the funeral should be fitting for Christian worship. One church policy indicates that only sacred music is allowed at the funeral and that the guidance of the clergy in selecting music is expected.[2]

FLOWERS

A church may choose to limit the number of flower arrangements that may be brought into the church for a funeral. It may be limited to the flowers intended for the altar or to a blanket of flowers on the coffin and a spray on either end. Flowers can help express the love and sympathy of friends and, in a limited amount, can add to the beauty of the worship service. Florists and funeral directors should be informed of the policy regulating the use of flowers.

MEMORIALS AND WILLS

The church may wish to encourage the giving of memorials at the time of death. The procedure to follow should be indicated. The wisdom of having one's will in good order is also an aspect of Christian stewardship. The church may wish to encourage the inclusion of one's church and other charities in the will.

THE FUNERAL PALL

The use of a pall symbolizes that there is no distinction between persons at death. It also symbolizes the protecting love of God that enfolds and keeps from harm his children

2. For more discussion of funeral music, see Chapter 4. For music suggestions, see Appendix 1.

in time of need. If the church owns and advocates the use of a pall, this should be mentioned in the policy statement. White is the color for celebration, but it soils easily. A purple pall is more practical.

RITUALS OF FRATERNAL ORDERS

When fraternal orders are asked by the family to conduct their rituals, this should be done *before* the church service, either at the home, at the funeral home, or at the fraternal meeting place. If fraternal rites are conducted at the graveside, they should *precede* the Christian committal service.

MILITARY HONORS

The minister may secure a copy of the procedure for a military funeral from a chaplain or military cemetery official in order to become familiar with the service. The cleric and the officer in command of the military detail should confer before the service as to proper arrangements for the service, particularly the committal rites. The national flag may be substituted for the funeral pall.

CELEBRATION OF THE LORD'S SUPPER

The celebration of the Lord's Supper, when permitted by a church's tradition, may be held either at the funeral service or at another time. This practice of the early Christians can be a means of strengthening the bereaved and of affirming Christ's victory over death and his living presence with believers in the communion of the saints.

Announcements by Funeral Directors

When it is necessary to announce the time and place of the interment, this should be done by the minister, not by the funeral director. Nor should any public statement be made by the funeral director at the grave regarding perpetual care or other provisions.

Committal Service

The recommendation of the church regarding the time of the committal service, whether before or after the worship service, may be indicated. Some churches recommend that the coffin be lowered to its final resting place before the committal service. This denotes the finality of death.

Costs

Most churches make available the use of their facilities and their clergy for funerals at no cost. When this is the case it should be so indicated in a funeral policy. And whether funeral establishments do or do not make additional charges for a church funeral should also be stated.

Honoraria for Clergy

The funeral statement should make it clear that the clergy *do not charge* for funeral services when the deceased was a member of the church. One denomination makes this emphatically certain in its book of worship, saying that the pastor shall not accept an honorarium for this service when the deceased was a member of that parish. This may be interpreted to mean that the pastor is also not to accept honoraria for the funerals of nonmembers, though a minister who is often called upon to conduct services for nonmembers may feel it proper to negotiate a fee.

The policy statement of another denomination indicates that if the family wishes to send an offering to the church or an honorarium to the minister, it may do so. When the minister has incurred unusual travel expenses related to the funeral, it is acceptable to be reimbursed.

The reason for returning honoraria or giving them to a charity in memory of the deceased is simply that ministers should not be paid for doing what they receive a salary to do as ministers of the gospel. The church's policy regarding an honorarium or fee for the minister of music or church organist should also be stated.

Some funeral establishments make it a practice to include a fee for the minister's services in the bill to the family. In some rare instances this has been done and the ministers were not made aware that the families had been billed, nor did they receive the honoraria. A policy statement may indicate that no such fee is to be collected.

Where there are many elderly people who die without church connections, the minister may be called on to conduct a great number of funeral services for such folk. The minister or the ministers of the community should negotiate with the funeral directors of the community regarding sharing the duty of performing such funerals and should negotiate appropriate fees. The fee should take into consideration time involved for both the funeral service and grief counseling with the family in the weeks that follow.

Traditional professional courtesy among ministers calls

for ministers to conduct funeral services for other clergy and their immediate family gratis. However, reimbursement for travel and entertainment expenses incurred may be accepted.

By definition, an honorarium is a payment for professional services on which custom forbids any price to be set. A policy statement should clarify this for the family of the deceased, the funeral director, and the members of the congregation.

PART II

FUNERAL LITURGIES

A UNITED METHODIST SERVICE

A Service of Death and Resurrection

Concerning the Service

The service should be held in the church if at all possible, and at a time when members of the congregation can be present.

This order is intended for use with the body of the deceased present, but it can be adapted for use at memorial services or other occasions.

The coffin remains closed throughout the service and thereafter. It may be covered with a pall.

Members of the deceased's family, friends, members of the congregation are strongly encouraged to share in conducting the service.

Optional parts of the service are in brackets []. Parts in boldface type are to be said or sung by the people.

Part or all of the committal service may be included in the church service as indicated.

Orders of Service

Gathering of the People

The pastor may welcome the family.
Music for worship may be offered while the people gather.
Songs of faith may be sung any time during the gathering.
If the coffin is already in place, the pastor opens the service with the following sentences. If not, it may be carried into the place of worship in procession, the pastor going before it and saying the sentences. The congregation stands.

The Word of Grace

Jesus said, I am the Resurrection and I am Life. Those who believe in me, even though they die, yet shall they live, and whoever lives and believes in me shall never die. I am Alpha and Omega, the beginning and the end, the first and the last. I died, and behold I am alive forever more, and I hold the keys of hell and death. Because I live, you shall live also.

Greeting

Friends, we have gathered here to praise God and to witness to our faith as we celebrate the life of (*name*). We come together in grief, acknowledging our human loss. May God search our hearts, that in pain we may find comfort, in sorrow hope, in death resurrection.

The following sentences may be added immediately after the Greeting if they have not been used earlier at the placing of the pall on the coffin.

Dying, Christ destroyed our death.

50

Rising, Christ restored our life.

Christ will come again in glory.

As in baptism (*name*) put on Christ, so in Christ may (*name*) be clothed with glory.

Here and now, dear friends, we are God's children.

What we shall be has not yet been revealed. But we know that when he appears we shall be like him, for we shall see him as he is.

Those who have this hope purify themselves as Christ is pure.

Hymn or Song

Prayer

The following or other prayers may be offered, in unison if desired. Petition for God's help, thanksgiving for the communion of saints, confession of sin and assurance of pardon are appropriate here.

Pastor: The Lord be with you.
People: And also with you.

Pastor: Let us pray.
O God, who gave us birth,
you are ever more ready to hear than we are to pray.
You know our needs before we ask, and our ignorance in asking.
Give to us now your grace,
that as we shrink before the mystery of death
we may see the light of eternity.
Speak to us once more your solemn message of life and of death.

51

Help us to live as those who are prepared to die.
And when our summons comes,
may we die as those who go forth to live,
so that living or dying, our life may be in you,
and nothing in life or in death will be able to
separate us from your great love in Christ Jesus
our Lord. Amen.

and/or

Eternal God, we praise you for the great company
of all those who have finished their course in faith
and now rest from their labor.
We praise you for those dear to us
whom we name in our hearts before you.
We praise you for your child *(name)*,
whom you have taken to yourself.
Grant peace to their souls.
Let perpetual light shine upon them.
And help us so to believe where we have not seen,
that your presence may lead us through our years,
and bring us at last with them into the joy of your
home not made with hands but eternal in the heavens;
through Jesus Christ our Lord. Amen.

and/or

Holy God, before you our hearts are open
and from you no secrets are hidden.
We bring to you now our shame and sorrow
    for our sins.
We have forgotten that our life is from you
    and unto you.
We have neither sought nor done your will.

We have not been truthful in our hearts,
in our speech, in our lives.
We have not loved as we ought to love.
Help us and heal us, we pray.
Raise us from our sins into a better life,
that we may end our days in peace
trusting in your kindness unto the end;
through Jesus Christ our Lord,
who lives and reigns with you in the unity
    of the Holy Spirit,
one God now and forever. Amen.

Pardon

Who is in a position to condemn?
Only Christ, Christ who died for us, who rose for
us, who reigns at God's right hand and prays for us.
Thanks be to God who gives us the victory
through our Lord Jesus Christ.

Psalm 130

Said or sung by the people, standing:
Out of depths I cry unto thee, O Lord!
    Lord, hear my cry.
Let thine ears be attentive
    to the voice of my supplication.
If thou, Lord, should mark iniquities
    Lord, who could stand?
But there is forgiveness with thee,
    that thou may be feared.
I wait for the Lord, my soul waits,
    and in his word do I hope.
My soul waits for the Lord

more than those who watch for the morning.
O Israel, hope in the Lord!
    For with the Lord is great mercy.
With him is plenteous redemption,
    and he will redeem Israel from all their sins.

Proclamation and Praise

Scripture Readings

*Lections are from the Old and New Testaments. A short prayer
for illumination may precede the lections. Preferably, a lec-
tion from one of the Gospels should conclude the readings.
It may be read from the midst of the congregation. Lay
readers may be selected.*

Old Testament   *(Arrangement of verses may be altered.)*

Preferred: Isaiah 40:1-6, 8-11, 28-31

Recommended: Exodus 14:5-14, 19-31
    Isaiah 43:1-3*a*, 5-7, 13, 15, 18-19, 25; 44:6, 8*a*
    Isaiah 55:1-3, 6-13
    Psalms 42, 43, 46, 90, 91, 103, 116, 121, 139, 145, 146

Psalm 23

Sung or said by the people, standing.
The Lord is my Shepherd; I shall not want.
He maketh me to lie down in green pastures:
    he leadeth me beside the still waters.

He restoreth my soul:
    he leadeth me in the paths of righteousness
    for his name's sake.
Yea, though I walk through the valley of the
    shadow of death,
    I will fear no evil:
    for thou art with me;
    thy rod and thy staff they comfort me.
Thou preparest a table before me
    in the presence of mine enemies:
    thou anointest my head with oil:
    my cup runneth over.
Surely goodness and mercy shall follow me
    all the days of my life:
    and I will dwell in the house of the Lord for ever.

Epistle   *(Arrangement of verses may be altered.)*

Preferred: I Corinthians 15:1-8, 12-20, 35-44, 53-55, 57-58
    Revelation 21:1-7, 22-27; 22:1-15

Recommended: Romans 8:1-2, 5-6, 10-11, 14-19, 22-28, 31-
    32, 35-39
    II Corinthians 4:5-18
    Ephesians 1:15-23; 2:1, 4-10
    I Peter 1:3-9, 13, 21-25
    Revelation 7:2-3, 9-17

Gospel   *(Arrangement of verses may be altered.)*

Preferred: John 14:1-10*a*, 15-21, 25-27

Recommended: Luke 24:13-35
   John 11:1-5, 20-27, 32-35, 38-44

Sermon

*A brief sermon may be preached, proclaiming the gospel in the
   face of death. It may lead into or include the following acts of
   naming and witness. These should be concluded with a hymn.*

Naming

*The life and death of the deceased may be gathered up by the
   reading of a memorial or appropriate statement, or in other
   ways, by the pastor or others.*

Witness

*Family, friends, members of the congregation may briefly voice
   their thankfulness to God for the grace they have received
   in the life of the deceased, and their Christian faith and joy.
   Signs of faith, hope, and love may be exchanged.*

Hymn

Offering of Life

*If the Committal is to conclude this service, the Order of Com-
   mittal may be shortened and substituted for this section.*

Creed

*A congregation, standing, may be led in the Apostles' Creed. If
   it has not been preceded by, it may be followed by a hymn
   or musical response.*

I believe in God, the Father almighty,

creator of heaven and earth.
I believe in Jesus Christ, his only Son, our Lord.
He was conceived by the power of the Holy Spirit
    and born of the Virgin Mary.
He suffered under Pontius Pilate,
    was crucified, died, and was buried.
He descended to the dead.
On the third day he rose again.
He ascended into heaven,
    and is seated at the right hand of the Father.
He will come again to judge the living and the dead.
I believe in the Holy Spirit,
    the holy catholic Church,
    the communion of saints,
    the forgiveness of sins,
    the resurrection of the body,
    and the life everlasting. Amen.

Prayers

*The following or other prayers may be offered. They may take
the form of a pastoral prayer, a series of shorter prayers, or
a litany. Intercession, commendation of life, and thanksgiving are appropriate here, concluded with the Lord's Prayer.*

God of us all, your love never ends.
When all else fails, you still are God.
We pray to you for one another in our need,
and for all, anywhere, who mourn with us this day.
To those who doubt, give light;
    to those who are weak, strength;
to all who have sinned, mercy;

to all who sorrow, your peace.
Keep true in us the love with which we hold each other.
In all our ways we trust you.
And to you, with your Church on earth and in heaven,
we offer honor and glory, now and for ever. **Amen.**
O God, all that you have given us is yours.
As first you gave *(name)* to us
so now we give *(name)* back to you.

*Here the pastor, with other celebrants, standing near the coffin,
    may lay hands on it, continuing:*

Receive *(name)* into the arms of your mercy.
Raise *(name)* up with all your people.
Receive us also, our selves, our souls, our bodies,
    and raise us into a new life.
Help us so to love and serve you in this world
that we may enter into your joy in the world to come.
    Amen.

Holy Communion

*The pastor may administer the Sacrament to all present who
    wish to share at the Lord's Table, using the Order [found
    below]. Otherwise the service continues with the following.*

Prayer of Thanksgiving

God of love, we thank you for all the happiness
with which you have blessed us even to this day:
for the gift of life; for home and friends;
for health and strength;
for work, and nature, and beauty;
for our baptism and place in your Church

with all who have faithfully lived and died.
More than all else we thank you for Jesus
　who knew our griefs,
who died our death and rose for our sake,
and who lives and prays for us.
As he taught us, so now we pray.

The Lord's Prayer

Our Father in heaven, hallowed be your Name,
　your kingdom come, your will be done,
　　on earth as in heaven.
Give us today our daily bread.
Forgive us our sins
　as we forgive those who sin against us.
Save us from the time of trial, and deliver us from evil.
For the kingdom, the power, and the glory are yours,
　now and for ever. Amen.

or

Our Father, who art in heaven, hallowed be thy Name,
　thy kingdom come, thy will be done,
　　on earth as it is in heaven.
Give us this day our daily bread.
And forgive us our trespasses,
　as we forgive those who trespass against us.
And lead us not into temptation, but deliver us
　from evil.
for thine is the kingdom, and the power, and the glory,
forever. Amen.

Hymn

Dismissal and Blessing

The pastor, facing the people, may say one or more of the
following, or other words of dismissal and blessing.

Now may the God of Peace
who brought again from the dead our Lord Jesus,
the great Shepherd of the sheep,
by the blood of the eternal covenant,
equip you with everything good
    that you may do his will,
working in you that which is pleasing in his sight,
through Jesus Christ;
to whom be glory for ever and ever. **Amen.**

    The peace of God which passes all
understanding keep your hearts and minds
    in the knowledge
    and love of God,
and of his Son Jesus Christ our Lord.
And the blessing of God almighty,
the Father, Son, and Holy Spirit,
be among you and remain with you always. **Amen.**

    Now may the Father
from whom every family in heaven and on earth is
named, according to the riches of his glory,
grant you to be strengthened with might
through his Spirit in your inner being,
that Christ may dwell in your hearts through faith;
that you, being rooted and grounded in love,
may be able to comprehend with all the saints

what is the breadth and length and height and
depth, and to know the love of Christ
    which surpasses knowledge,
that you may be filled with all the fullness of God.
Now to him who by the power at work in us
is able to do far more abundantly than all we ask or
think, to him be glory in the church and in Christ
Jesus to all generations, for ever and ever. **Amen.**

Recessional

An Order for Holy Communion

*This may be included following the prayers in the Order of
    Service, or before a common meal following the service, or
    with the family at some time following the service. If included,
    it replaces the Prayer of Thanksgiving and the Lord's Prayer.*

*The bread and wine are brought to the table, or uncovered if
    already in place. The pastor makes any necessary prepara-
    tion of the elements and then prays the following or another
    version of the Great Thanksgiving.*

Pastor: The Lord be with you.
People: **And also with you.**
Pastor: Lift up your hearts.
People: **We lift them to the Lord.**
Pastor: Let us give thanks to the Lord our God.
People: **It is right to give him thanks and praise.**
Pastor: Creator and Sovereign of the universe,
it is right that we should always and everywhere
give you thanks and praise,

through Jesus Christ our Lord,
who rose victorious from the dead,
and comforts us with the blessed hope
    of everlasting life.
For your faithful people life is changed, not ended;
and when our mortal body lies in death,
there is prepared for us a dwelling place
    eternal in the heavens.
Therefore, with your people in all ages
    and the whole company of heaven
    we join in the song of unending praise.

Pastor and people: **Holy, holy, holy Lord, God**
    of power and might,
heaven and earth are full of your glory.
    Hosanna in the highest.
Blessed is he who comes in the name of the Lord.
    Hosanna in the highest.

Pastor: Blessed are you, Lord our God,
because you loved the world so much
    you gave your only Son Jesus Christ to be our Savior.
He suffered and died for the sin of the world.
You raised him from the dead
    that we, too, might have new life.
He ascended to be with you in glory,
    and by the power of your Holy Spirit
    is with us always.
On the night he offered himself up for us
he took bread, gave thanks to you, broke it,
    gave it to his disciples, and said:
"Take, eat; this is my body which is given for you.

Do this in remembrance of me."
When supper was over,
he took the cup, gave thanks to you,
    gave it to his disciples, and said:
"Drink from this, all of you;
    this cup is the new covenant sealed by my blood,
    poured out for you and many,
    for the forgiveness of sins.
Whenever you drink it, do this in remembrance of me."
Therefore,
    in remembrance of all your mighty acts
    in Jesus Christ,
we ask you to accept
    this our sacrifice of praise and thanksgiving,
    which we offer in union with Christ's offering for
    us as a living and holy surrender of ourselves.
Send the power of your Holy Spirit on us
    and on these gifts,
that the sharing of this bread and wine
    may be for us a sharing
    in the body and blood of Christ,
that we may be one body in him, cleansed by his blood,
and that we may faithfully serve him in the world,
    looking forward to his coming in final victory.
Renew our communion with all your saints,
    especially (*name*) and all those most dear to us.
May we run with perseverance the race that is set
        before us,
    and with them receive the unfading crown of glory,
    through your Son Jesus Christ.

Pastor and people: **Through him, with him, and in him,**

in the unity of the Holy Spirit,
all glory and honor is yours, almighty God,
    now and for ever. Amen.

Our Father in heaven,
    hallowed be your Name,
    your kingdom come,
    your will be done,
    on earth as in heaven.
Give us today our daily bread.
Forgive us our sins
    as we forgive those
    who sin against us.
Save us from the time of trial,
    and deliver us from evil.
For the kingdom, the power,
    and the glory are yours,
    now and for ever. Amen.

or

Our Father, who art in heaven,
    hallowed be thy Name,
    thy kingdom come,
    thy will be done,
    on earth as it is in heaven.
Give us this day our daily bread.
And forgive us our trespasses,
    as we forgive those
    who trespass against us.
And lead us not into temptation,
    but deliver us from evil.
For thine is the kingdom,

and the power, and the glory,
forever. Amen.

The pastor breaks the bread.
    The bread and wine are given to the people with these or
    other words being exchanged:

The body of Christ, given for you. **Amen.**
The blood of Christ, given for you. **Amen.**

During the giving of the bread and wine, hymns or songs of
    praise may be sung.

Then follows the Dismissal and Blessing.

An Order of Committal

This service is intended primarily for burial in the ground.
    However, it can be adapted for cremation or the interment
    of ashes, for burial above ground or at sea, or when the body
    is donated for medical purposes.
The pastor should preside.
Prayers and lections appropriate for a service for a child or
    youth, or for other distinctive occasions, may be read.

When the people have gathered, the pastor says one or more of
    the following:

In the midst of life we are in death;
from whom can we seek help?
Our help is in the name of the Lord,
who made heaven and earth.

He who raised Jesus Christ from the dead
will give life to your mortal bodies also
through his Spirit which dwells in you.

Behold, I tell you a mystery!
We shall not all die, but we shall all be changed.
This perishable nature must put on the imperishable,
this mortal the immortal.
Then shall come to pass the saying,
"Death is swallowed up in victory."
"O death, where is your sting?
O grave, where is your victory?"
Thanks be to God who gives us the victory
through our Lord Jesus Christ.

Therefore my heart is glad and my spirit rejoices.
My body also shall rest in hope.
You, Lord, will show me the path of life.
In your presence is fullness of joy,
and at your right hand are pleasures forever more.

The following prayer is offered:

Let us pray.
O God, you have ordered this wonderful world
    and know all things in earth and in heaven.
Give us such faith that by day and by night,
at all times and in all places,
we may without fear commit ourselves
    and those dear to us
to your never-failing love,
in this life and in the life to come. **Amen.**

One of the following or other Scriptures may be read:

Blessed be the God and Father of our Lord Jesus Christ! By his great mercy we have been born anew to a living hope through the resurrection of Jesus Christ from the dead, and to an inheritance which is imperishable, unde-filed and unfading, kept in heaven for you. In this you rejoice, though now for a little while you may have to suffer various trials so that the genuineness of your faith may prove itself worthy at the revelation of Jesus Christ. Without having seen him, yet you love him; though you do not now see him, you believe in him and rejoice with unutterable and exalted joy. As the outcome of your faith you obtain the salvation of your souls.

Jesus said: The hour has come for the son of man to be glorified. Truly, truly, I say to you, unless a grain of wheat falls into the earth and dies, it remains alone; but if it dies it bears much fruit. He who loves his life loses it, and he who hates his life in this world will keep it unto life eternal. If anyone serves me, he must follow me; and where I am, there shall my servant be also. If anyone serves me, the Father will honor him.

Standing at the head of the coffin and facing it, while earth is cast upon it as the coffin is lowered into the grave, the pastor says the following:

Almighty God, into your hands we commend your child (*name*), in sure and certain hope of resurrection to eternal life through Jesus Christ our Lord. **Amen.**
    This body we commit to the ground (*or* the elements,

or its resting place, *or* the deep), earth to earth, ashes to ashes, dust to dust. Blessed are the dead who die in the Lord. Henceforth, says the Spirit, they rest from their labors and their works follow them.

One or more of the following or other prayers is offered:

Let us pray.
Gracious God,
We thank you for those we love but see no more.
Receive into your arms your servant (*name*), and grant that increasing in knowledge and love of you, *(name)* may go from strength to strength in service in your heavenly kingdom; through Jesus Christ our Lord. **Amen.**

Almighty God,
look with pity upon the sorrow of your servants for whom we pray.
Help them amidst things they cannot understand to trust in your care.
Bless them and keep them.
Make your face to shine upon them
and be gracious to them.
Lift up your countenance upon them
and give them peace. **Amen.**

O God, whose days are without end,
make us deeply aware of the shortness and uncertainty of our human life.
Raise us from sin into love and goodness,
that when we depart this life we may rest in Christ
and receive the blessing he has promised

to those who love and serve him,
"Come, you blessed of my Father, receive the kingdom
prepared for you from the foundation of the world."
Grant this, merciful Father, through Jesus Christ
our Mediator and Redeemer. **Amen.**

O Lord, support us all the day long of our troubled life,
until the shadows lengthen and the evening comes and
the busy world is hushed, and the fever of life is over
and our work is done.
Then in your mercy grant us a safe lodging
and a holy rest, and peace at the last;
through Jesus Christ our Lord. **Amen.**

Eternal God, you have shared with us the life of *(name)*.
Before *(name)* was ours, *(name)* is yours.
For all that *(name)* has given us to make us what we
are, for that of *(name)* which lives and grows in each of
us, and for *(name's)* life that in your love will never
end, we give thanks.
As now we offer *(name)* back into your arms,
we pray for comfort in our loneliness,
strength in our weakness,
and courage to face the future unafraid.
Draw those of us who remain in this life
    closer to one another,
make us faithful to serve one another,
and give us to know that peace and joy
    which is eternal life;
through Jesus Christ our Lord. **Amen.**

The Lord's Prayer may follow:

Our Father in heaven,
hallowed be your Name,
   your kingdom come,
   your will be done,
    on earth as in heaven.
Give us today our daily bread.
Forgive us our sins
   as we forgive those
   who sin against us.
Save us from the time of trial,
   and deliver us from evil.
For the kingdom, the power,
   and the glory are yours,
   now and for ever. Amen.

or

Our Father, who are in heaven,
   hallowed be thy Name,
   thy kingdom come,
   thy will be done,
    on earth as it is in heaven.
Give us this day our daily bread.
And forgive us our trespasses,
   as we forgive those
   who trespass against us.
And lead us not into temptation,
   but deliver us from evil.
For thine is the kingdom,
   and the power, and the glory,
   forever. Amen.

A hymn or song may be sung.

The pastor dismisses the people with the following or another blessing:

Now unto him who is able to keep you from falling,
and present you faultless before the presence of
   his glory
with exceeding joy,
to the only God our Savior
be glory and majesty, dominion and power,
through Jesus Christ our Lord,
both now and forever more. **Amen.**

8

AN EPISCOPAL SERVICE

THE BURIAL OF THE DEAD: RITE TWO

Concerning the Service

The death of a member of the Church should be reported as soon as possible to, and arrangements for the funeral should be made in consultation with, the Minister of the Congregation.

Baptized Christians are properly buried from the church. The service should be held at a time when the congregation has opportunity to be present.

The coffin is to be closed before the service, and it remains closed thereafter. It is appropriate that it be covered with a pall or other suitable covering.

If necessary, or if desired, all or part of the service of Committal may be said in the church. If preferred, the Committal service may take place before the service in the church. It may also be used prior to cremation.

A priest normally presides at the service. It is appropriate that the bishop, when present, preside at the Eucharist and pronounce the commendation.

From *The Book of Common Prayer of the Episcopal Church.*

It is desirable that the Lesson from the Old Testament, and the Epistle, be read by lay persons.

When the services of a priest cannot be obtained, a deacon or lay reader may preside at the service.

At the burial of a child, the passages from Lamentations, I John, and John 6, together with Psalm 23, are recommended.

It is customary that the celebrant meet the body and go before it into the church or towards the grave.

The anthems at the beginning of the service are sung or said as the body is borne into the church, or during the entrance of the ministers, or by the celebrant standing in the accustomed place.

Order of Service

All stand while one or more of the following anthems are sung or said. A hymn, psalm, or some other suitable anthem may be sung instead.

I am Resurrection and I am Life, says the Lord.
Whoever has faith in me shall have life,
even though he die.
And everyone who has life,
and has committed himself to me in faith,
shall not die for ever.

As for me, I know that my Redeemer lives
and that at the last he will stand upon the earth.
After my awaking, he will raise me up;
and in my body I shall see God.
I myself shall see, and my eyes behold him
who is my friend and not a stranger.

For none of us has life in himself,
and none becomes his own master when he dies.
For if we have life, we are alive in the Lord,
and if we die, we die in the Lord.
So, then, whether we live or die,
we are the Lord's possession.

Happy from now on
are those who die in the Lord!
So it is, says the Spirit,
for they rest from their labors.

Or else this anthem:

In the midst of life we are in death;
from whom can we seek help?
From you alone, O Lord,
who by our sins are justly angered.

**Holy God, Holy and Mighty,
Holy and merciful Savior,
deliver us not into the bitterness of eternal death.**

Lord, you know the secrets of our hearts;
shut not your ears to our prayers
but spare us, O Lord.

**Holy God, Holy and Mighty,
Holy and merciful Savior,
deliver us not into the bitterness of eternal death.**

O worthy and eternal Judge,

do not let the pains of death
turn us away from you at our last hour.

**Holy God, Holy and Mighty,
Holy and merciful Savior,
deliver us not into the bitterness of eternal death.**

When all are in place, the Celebrant may address the congregation, acknowledging briefly the purpose of their gathering, and bidding their prayers for the deceased and the bereaved.

The Celebrant then says,

The Lord be with you.
People: **And also with you.**
Celebrant: Let us pray.

Silence may be kept; after which the Celebrant says one of the following Collects:

At the Burial of an Adult

O God, who by the glorious resurrection of your Son Jesus Christ destroyed death, and brought life and immortality to light: Grant that your servant (*name*), being raised with him, may know the strength of his presence, and rejoice in his eternal glory; who with you and the Holy Spirit lives and reigns, one God, for ever and ever. **Amen.**

or

O God, whose mercies cannot be numbered: Accept our

prayers on behalf of your servant (*name*), and grant *him* an entrance into the land of light and joy, in the fellowship of your saints; through Jesus Christ our Lord, who lives and reigns with you and the Holy Spirit, one God, now and for ever. **Amen.**

or

O God of grace and glory, we remember before you this day our brother (sister) (*name*). We thank you for giving *him* to us, *his* family and friends, to know and to love as a companion on our earthly pilgrimage. In your boundless compassion, console us who mourn. Give us faith to see in death the gate of eternal life, so that in quiet confidence we may continue our course on earth, until, by your call, we are reunited with those who have gone before; through Jesus Christ our Lord. **Amen.**

At the Burial of a Child

O God, whose beloved Son took children into his arms and blessed them: Give us grace to entrust (*name*) to your neverfailing care and love, and bring us all to your heavenly kingdom; through Jesus Christ our Lord, who lives and reigns with you and the Holy Spirit, one God, now and for ever. **Amen.**

The Celebrant may add the following prayer:

Most merciful God, whose wisdom is beyond our under-standing: deal graciously with (*name*) in *their* grief. Surround *them* with your love, that *they* may not be over-whelmed by *their* loss, but have confidence in your goodness, and strength to meet the days to come; through Jesus Christ our Lord. **Amen.**

The Liturgy of the Word

The people sit.
One or more of the following passages from Holy Scripture is read. If there is to be a Communion, a passage from the Gospel always concludes the readings.

From the Old Testament

Isaiah 25:6-9 (He will swallow up death for ever)
Isaiah 61:1-3 (To comfort those who mourn)
Lamentations 3:22-26, 31-33 (The Lord is good to those who wait for him)
Wisdom 3:1-5, 9 (The souls of the righteous are in the hands of God)
Job 19:21-27*a* (I know that my Redeemer lives)

A suitable psalm, hymn, or canticle may follow. The following Psalms are appropriate: 42:1-7, 46, 90:1-12, 121, 130, 139:1-11.

From the New Testament

Romans 8:14-19, 34-35, 37-39 (The glory that shall be revealed)
1 Corinthians 15:20-26, 35-38, 42-44, 53-58 (The imperishable body)
2 Corinthians 4:16–5:9 (Things that are unseen are eternal)

1 John 3:1-2 (We shall be like him)
Revelation 7:9-17 (God will wipe away every tear)
Revelation 21:2-7 (Behold, I make all things new)

A suitable psalm, hymn, or canticle may follow. The following
Psalms are appropriate: 23, 27, 106:1-5, 116.

The Gospel

Then all standing, the Deacon or Minister appointed reads the
Gospel, first saying:

The Holy Gospel of our Lord Jesus Christ according to
John.

People: **Glory to you, Lord Christ.**

John 5:24-27 (He who believes has everlasting life)
John 6:37-40 (All that the Father gives me will come
    to me)
John 10:11-16 (I am the good shepherd)
John 11:21-27 (I am the resurrection and the life)
John 14:1-6 (In my Father's house are many rooms)

At the end of the Gospel, the Reader says:

The Gospel of the Lord.

People: **Praise to you, Lord Christ.**

Here there may be a homily by the Celebrant, or a member of
the family, or a friend.

The Apostles' Creed may then be said, all standing. The Celebrant may introduce the Creed with these or similar words.

In the assurance of eternal life given at Baptism, let us proclaim our faith and say,

Celebrant and People:

I believe in God, the Father almighty,
    creator of heaven and earth.

I believe in Jesus Christ, his only Son, our Lord.
    He was conceived by the power of the Holy Spirit
        and born of the Virgin Mary.
    He suffered under Pontius Pilate,
        was crucified, died, and was buried.
    He was descended to the dead.
    On the third day he rose again.
    He ascended into heaven,
        and is seated at the right hand of the Father.
    He will come again to judge the living and the dead.

I believe in the Holy Spirit,
    the holy catholic Church,
    the communion of saints,
    the forgiveness of sins,
    the resurrection of the body,
    and the life everlasting. Amen.

If there is not to be a Communion, the Lord's Prayer is said here, and the service continues with the Prayers of the People, or with one or more suitable prayers.

For our brother (sister) (*name*), let us pray to our Lord Jesus Christ who said, "I am Resurrection and I am Life."

Lord, you consoled Martha and Mary in their distress; draw near to us who mourn for (*name*), and dry the tears of those who weep.
Hear us, Lord.
You wept at the grave of Lazarus, your friend; comfort us in our sorrow.
Hear us, Lord.
You raised the dead to life; give to our brother (sister) eternal life.
Hear us, Lord.
You promised paradise to the thief who repented; bring our brother (sister) to the joys of heaven.
Hear us, Lord.
Our brother (sister) was washed in Baptism and anointed with the Holy Spirit; give *him* fellowship with all your saints.
Hear us, Lord.
He was nourished with your Body and Blood; grant *him* a place at the table in your heavenly kingdom.
Hear us, Lord.
Comfort us in our sorrows at the death of our brother (sister); let our faith be our consolation, and eternal life our hope.

Silence may be kept.
The Celebrant concludes with one of the following or some other prayer:

Lord Jesus Christ, we commend to you our brother (sister) (*name*), who was reborn by water and the Spirit in Holy Baptism. Grant that *his* death may recall to us your victory over death, and be an occasion for us to renew our trust in your Father's love. Give us, we pray, the faith to follow where you have led the way; and where you live and reign with the Father and the Holy Spirit, to the ages of ages. **Amen.**

or

Father of all, we pray to you for (*name*), and for all those whom we love but see no longer. Grant to them eternal rest. Let light perpetual shine upon them. May *his* soul and the souls of all the departed, through the mercy of God, rest in peace. **Amen.**

When there is no Communion, the service continues with the Commendation, or with the Committal.
If the body is not present, the service continues with the (blessing and) dismissal.
Unless the Committal follows immediately in the church, the following Commendation is used.

The Commendation

The Celebrant and other ministers take their places at the body.
This anthem, or some other suitable anthem, or a hymn, may be sung or said:

Give rest, O Christ, to your servant(s) with your saints,
where sorrow and pain are no more,
neither sighing, but life everlasting.

You only are immortal, the creator and maker of mankind; and we are mortal, formed of the earth, and to earth shall we return. For so did you ordain when you created me, saying, "You are dust, and to dust you shall return." All of us go down to the dust; yet even at the grave we make our song: Alleluia, alleluia, alleluia.

Give rest, O Christ, to your servant(s) with your saints, where sorrow and pain are no more, neither sighing, but life everlasting.

The Celebrant, facing the body, says:

Into your hands, O merciful Savior, we commend your servant (*name*). Acknowledge, we humbly beseech you, a sheep of your own fold, a lamb of your own flock, a sinner of your own redeeming. Receive *him* into the arms of your mercy, into the blessed rest of everlasting peace, and into the glorious company of the saints in light. **Amen.**

The Celebrant, or the Bishop if present, may then bless the people, and a Deacon or other Minister may dismiss them, saying:

Let us go forth in the name of Christ.
Thanks be to God.

As the body is borne from the church, a hymn or one or more of these anthems may be sung or said:

Christ is risen from the dead, trampling down death by death, and giving life to those in the tomb.

The Sun of Righteousness is gloriously risen, giving light to those who sat in darkness and in the shadow of death.

The Lord will guide our feet into the way of peace, having taken away the sin of the world.

Christ will open the kingdom of heaven to all who believe in his Name, saying, Come, O blessed of my Father; inherit the kingdom prepared for you.

Into paradise may the angels lead you. At your coming may the martyrs receive you, and bring you into the holy city Jerusalem.

or one of these Canticles:

The Song of Zechariah, *Benedictus*
The Song of Simeon, *Nunc dimittis*
Christ our Passover, *Pascha nostrum*

The Committal

The following anthem is sung or said:

Everyone the Father gives to me will come to me;
I will never turn away anyone who believes in me.

He who raised Jesus Christ from the dead
will also give new life to our mortal bodies
through his indwelling Spirit.

My heart, therefore, is glad, and my spirit rejoices;
my body also shall rest in hope.

You will show me the path of life;
in your presence there is fullness of joy,
and in your right hand are pleasures for evermore.

*Then, while earth is cast upon the coffin, the Celebrant says
    these words:*

In sure and certain hope of the resurrection to eternal life
through our Lord Jesus Christ, we commend to Almighty
God our *brother* (*name*), and we commit *his* body to the
ground;* earth to earth, ashes to ashes, dust to dust. The
Lord bless *him* and keep *him,* the Lord make his face to
shine upon *him* and be gracious to *him,* the Lord lift up
his countenance upon *him* and give *him* peace. **Amen.**

Celebrant: The Lord be with you.
People: **And also with you.**
Celebrant: Let us pray.

Celebrant and People:
Our Father, who art in heaven,
    hallowed be thy Name,
    thy kingdom come,
    thy will be done,
        on earth as it is in heaven.
Give us this day our daily bread.
And forgive us our trespasses,
    as we forgive those
        who trespass against us.

And lead us not into temptation,
    but deliver us from evil.
For thine is the kingdom,
    and the power, and the glory,
    for ever and ever. Amen.

or

Our Father in heaven,
    hallowed be your Name,
    your kingdom come,
    your will be done,
        on earth as in heaven.
Give us today our daily bread.
Forgive us our sins
    as we forgive those
        who sin against us.
Save us from the time of trial,
    and deliver us from evil.
For the kingdom, the power,
    and the glory are yours,
    now and for ever. Amen.

Other prayers may be added.
Then may be said:

Rest eternal grant to *him*, O Lord;
And let light perpetual shine upon *(him).*

May *his* soul, and the souls of all the departed,
through the mercy of God, rest in peace. **Amen.**

The Celebrant dismisses the people with these words:

Alleluia. Christ is risen.
People: **The Lord is risen indeed. Alleluia.**
Celebrant: Let us go forth in the name of Christ.
People: **Thanks be to God.**

or with the following:

The God of peace, who brought again from the dead our Lord Jesus Christ, the great Shepherd of the sheep, through the blood of the everlasting covenant: Make you perfect in every good work to do his will, working in you that which is well-pleasing in his sight; through Jesus Christ, to whom be glory for ever and ever. **Amen.**

9

A PRESBYTERIAN SERVICE

The Funeral:
A Service of Witness to the Resurrection

When death occurs, the pastor and other officers of the congregation should be informed as soon as possible, in order that they might provide appropriate consolation and support to the family and friends, and assist them in making arrangements for the funeral.

Except for compelling reasons, the service for a believing Christian is normally held in the church, at a time when the congregation can be present. When the deceased was not known to be a believer or had no connection with a church, then it is appropriate to hold the service elsewhere and to omit or adapt portions of it as seems fitting. The ceremonies and rites of fraternal, civic, or military organizations, if any, should occur at some other time and place.

Family members, friends, or members of the congregation may be invited by the minister to share in the service.

This order is intended for use with the body or ashes of the

---

deceased present, but it may be adapted for use as a
memorial service. The committal may follow or precede this
service, as preferred.

When the body is present, the coffin should be closed before the
service begins. It may be covered with a white funeral pall.

Placing of the Pall

A pall may be placed over the coffin at the time the body is
received at the entrance to the church, or, if there is to be a
procession, immediately before the procession.

As the pall is placed over the coffin by the pallbearers, the
minister says one of the following:

1   *Gal. 3:27*

For as many of you as were baptized into Christ
have clothed yourselves with Christ.

In *his/her* baptism N. was clothed with Christ;
in the day of Christ's coming,
he/she shall be clothed with glory.

2   *Rom. 6:3-5*

When we were baptized in Christ Jesus,
we were baptized into his death.
We were buried therefore with him by baptism into
    death,
so that, as Christ was raised from the dead by the glory
    of the Father,

we too might live a new life.
For if we have been united with Christ in a death like
  his,
we will certainly be united with him in a resurrection
  like his.

Appropriate music may be offered as the people gather.
All may stand as the minister(s) and other worship leaders enter.
If there is a procession into the place of worship, the minister
  leads it as the congregation sings a psalm or a hymn. Or,
  the minister may say or sing one or more of the sentences of
  scripture below, while leading the procession.
If the coffin or urn of ashes has already been brought in, the
  minister begins the service with one or more of the following,
  or similar sentences.

Sentences of Scripture

1   *Ps. 124:8*

Our help is in the name of the Lord,
who made heaven and earth.

2   *Rom. 6:3-5*

When we were baptized in Christ Jesus,
we were baptized into his death.
We were buried therefore with him by baptism into
  death,
so that, as Christ was raised from the dead by the glory
  of the Father,

we too might live a new life.
For if we have been united with Christ in a death like
   his,
we will certainly be united with him in a resurrection
   like his.

3   *John 11:25-26*

I am the resurrection and the life, says the Lord.
Those who believe in me, even though they die,
   shall live,
and everyone who lives and believes in me will never
   die.

4   *Rev. 21:6; 22:13; 1:17-18; John 14:19*

I am the Alpha and the Omega,
the beginning and the end,
the first and the last.
I was dead and behold I am alive forever and ever;
and I have the keys of Death and Hades.
Because I live, you also will live.

5   *Matt. 11:28*

Come to me, all you that are weary
and are carrying heavy burdens,
and I will give you rest.

6   *John 14:27*

Peace I leave with you;
my peace I give to you.
I do not give to you as the world gives.
Do not let your hearts be troubled,
And do not let them be afraid.

7   *Ps. 103:13; Isa. 66:13*

As a father has compassion for his children,
so the Lord has compassion for those who fear God.
As a mother comforts her child,
so I will comfort you, says the Lord.

8   *Deut. 33:27*

The eternal God is your dwelling place,
and underneath are the everlasting arms.

9   *Matt. 5:4*

Blessed are those who mourn,
for they will be comforted.

10   *2 Cor. 1:3-4*

Praise be to the God and Father of our Lord Jesus
     Christ,
the Father of mercies and God of all comfort,
who comforts us in all our sorrows,

so that we can comfort others in their sorrow,
with the consolation we have received from God.

11   *Rom. 14:8*

If we live, we live to the Lord;
and if we die, we die to the Lord;
so then, whether we live or whether we die,
we are the Lord's.

12   *Rev. 14:13*

Blessed are the dead who die in the Lord, says the Spirit.
They will rest from their labors,
and their deeds follow them.

Psalm, Hymn, or Spiritual

The congregation may sing a psalm, hymn of praise, or spiritual.

Prayer

The Lord be with you.
And also with you.
Let us pray.

After a brief silence, one of the following, or a similar prayer, is said.

1

Eternal God,
maker of heaven and earth:
You formed us from the dust of the earth,
and by your breath you gave us life.
We glorify you.

Jesus Christ,
the resurrection and the life:
You tasted death for all humanity,
and by rising from the grave
you opened the way to eternal life.
We praise you.

Holy Spirit,
author and giver of life:
You are the comforter of all who sorrow,
our sure confidence
and everlasting hope.
We worship you.

To you, O blessed Trinity,
be glory and honor, forever and ever.
Amen.

2

O God, who gave us birth,
you are ever more ready to hear than we are to pray.
You know our needs before we ask,
and our ignorance in asking.

Show us now your grace,
that as we face the mystery of death
we may see the light of eternity.

Speak to us once more your solemn message of life and
    of death.
Help us to live as those who are prepared to die.
and when our days here are ended,
enable us to die as those who go forth to live,
so that living or dying,
our life may be in Jesus Christ our risen Lord.
Amen.

3

Eternal God, we bless you for the great company
of all those who have kept the faith,
finished their race,
and who now rest from their labor.
We praise you for those dear to us
whom we name in our hearts before you. . . .
Especially we thank you for N.,
whom you have now received into your presence.

Help us to believe where we have not seen,
trusting you to lead us through our years.
Bring us at last with all your saints
into the joy of your home,
through Jesus Christ our Lord.
Amen.

4

Eternal God,
we acknowledge the uncertainty of our life on earth.
We are given a mere handful of days,
and our span of life seems nothing in your sight.
All flesh is as grass;
and all its beauty is like the flower of the field.
The grass withers, the flower fades;
but your word will stand forever.
In this is our hope,
for you are our God.
Even in the valley of the shadow of death,
you are with us.

O Lord, let us know our end
and the number of our days,
that we may learn how fleeting life is.
Turn your ear to our cry, and hear our prayer.
Do not be silent at our tears,
for we live as strangers before you,
wandering pilgrims as all our ancestors were.
But you are the same
and your years shall have no end.
Amen.

Confession and Pardon

A prayer of confession may be said.

Call to Confession

The minister says:

Let us now ask God to cleanse our hearts,
to redeem our memories,
and to renew our confidence in the goodness of God.

All confess their sin, using the following prayer:

Holy God, you see us as we are,
and know our inmost thoughts.
We confess that we are unworthy of your gracious care.
We forget that all life comes from you
and that to you all life returns.
We have not always sought or done your will.
We have not lived as your grateful children,
nor loved as Christ loved us.
Apart from you we are nothing.
Only your grace can sustain us.

Lord, in your mercy, forgive us,
heal us and make us whole.
Set us free from our sin,
and restore to us the joy of your salvation
now and forever.

Silent prayer may follow.

Declaration of Forgiveness

The minister declares the assurance of God's forgiving grace:

1   *Rom. 8:34; 2 Cor. 5:17*

Hear the good news!
Who is in a position to condemn?
Only Christ,
and Christ died for us,
Christ rose for us,
Christ reigns in power for us,
Christ prays for us.

Anyone who is in Christ
is a new creation.
The old life has gone;
a new life has begun.

Know that you are forgiven
and be at peace.
Amen.

2

The mercy of the Lord
is from everlasting to everlasting.
I declare to you, in the name of Jesus Christ,
you are forgiven.

May the God of mercy,
who forgives you all your sins,
strengthen you in all goodness,
and by the power of the Holy Spirit
keep you in eternal life.
Amen.

*Before the readings, the people may sing a thankful response to
    the mercy of God.*
The people may be seated.

Readings from Scripture

*Before the readings, one of the following, or another prayer for
    illumination, may be said by the reader:*

1

Source of all true wisdom,
calm the troubled waters of our hearts,
and still all other voices but your own,
that we may hear and obey
what you tell us in your Word,
through the power of your Spirit.
Amen.

2

Eternal God,
Your love for us is everlasting;
you alone can turn the shadow of death
into the brightness of the morning light.
Help us to turn to you with believing hearts.
In the stillness of this hour,
speak to us of eternal things,
so that, hearing the promises in scripture,
we may have hope and be lifted above our distress
into the peace of your presence;

through Jesus Christ our Lord.
Amen.

One or more selections from scripture are read.
It is appropriate that there be readings from both the Old and
New Testaments and that they include a reading from the
Gospels. A psalm or a canticle may be sung or read between
the readings.

Sermon

After the scriptures are read, their message may be proclaimed
in a brief sermon. Expressions of gratitude to God for the
life of the deceased may follow.

Affirmation of Faith

The congregation may stand and say or sing the Apostles' Creed
(which follows). Or the congregation may sing "We Praise
You, O God" instead of or following the creed. Or another
affirmation of faith may be said:

Let us confess the faith of our baptism, as we say:

I believe in God, the Father almighty,
creator of heaven and earth.

I believe in Jesus Christ, God's only Son, our Lord,
who was conceived by the Holy Spirit,
born of the Virgin Mary,
suffered under Pontius Pilate,
was crucified, died, and was buried;
he descended to the dead.

On the third day he rose again;
he ascended into heaven,
he is seated at the right hand of the Father,
and he will come again to judge the living
    and the dead.

I believe in the Holy Spirit,
the holy catholic church,
the communion of saints,
the forgiveness of sins,
the resurrection of the body,
and the life everlasting. Amen.

[Hymn]

A hymn of confident faith may be sung by the congregation.

Prayers of Thanksgiving, Supplication, and Intercession

One of the following, or a similar prayer, is offered.

1

O God of grace,
you have given us new and living hope in Jesus Christ.
We thank you that by dying
Christ destroyed the power of death,
and by rising from the grave
opened the way to eternal life.

Help us to know that because he lives,

we shall live also;
and that neither death nor life,
nor things present nor things to come
shall be able to separate us from your love
in Christ Jesus our Lord.
Amen.

2

O God,
before whom generations rise and pass away,
we praise you for all your servants
who, having lived this life in faith,
now live eternally with you.

Especially we thank you for your servant N.,
whose baptism is now complete in death.
We praise you for the gift of *his/her* life,
for all in *him/her* that was good and kind and faithful,
for the grace you gave *him/her,*
that kindled in *him/her* the love of your dear name,
and enabled *him/her* to serve you faithfully.

*Here mention may be made of the person's characteristics or
    service.*

We thank you that for *him/her* death is past and pain
    ended,
and that *he/she* has now entered the joy you have
    prepared;
through Jesus Christ our Lord.
Amen.

3

Almighty God,
in Jesus Christ you promised many rooms within
    your house.
Give us faith to see, beyond touch and sight,
some sure sign of your kingdom,
and, where vision fails,
to trust your love which never fails.
Lift heavy sorrow
and give us good hope in Jesus,
so we may bravely walk our earthly way,
and look forward to glad reunion in the life to come,
through Jesus Christ our Lord.
Amen.

4

For our *brother/sister* N.,
let us pray to our Lord Jesus Christ
who said, "I am the resurrection and the life."
Lord, you consoled Martha and Mary in their distress;
draw near to us who mourn for N.,
and dry the tears of those who weep.

Hear us, Lord.

You wept at the grave of Lazarus, your friend;
comfort us in our sorrow.

Hear us, Lord.

You raised the dead to life;
give to our *brother/sister* eternal life.

Hear us, Lord.

You promised paradise to the repentant thief;
bring N. to the joys of heaven.

Hear us, Lord.

Our *brother/sister* was washed in baptism
and anointed with the Holy Spirit;
give *him/her* fellowship with all your saints.

Hear us, Lord.

He/she was nourished at your table on earth;
welcome *him/her* at your table in the heavenly kingdom.

Hear us, Lord.

Comfort us in our sorrows at the death of N.;
let our faith be our consolation,
and eternal life our hope.
Amen.

5

At the death of a child:

Loving God,
you are nearest to us when we need you most.

In this hour of sorrow we turn to you,
trusting in your loving mercy.

We bless you for the gift of this child,
for *his/her* baptism into your church,
for the joy *he/she* gave all who knew *him/her*,
for the precious memories that will abide with us,
and for the assurance that *he/she* lives forever
in the joy and peace of your presence.
Amen.

6

At the death of a child:

O God,
your love cares for us in life
and watches over us in death.
We bless you for our Savior's joy in little children
and for the assurance that of such is the kingdom
    of heaven.
In our sorrow,
make us strong to commit ourselves, and those we love,
to your unfailing care.
In our perplexity,
help us to trust where we cannot understand.
In our loneliness,
may we remember N. in love,
trusting *him/her* to your keeping
until the eternal morning breaks;
through Jesus Christ our Lord.
Amen.

7

After a sudden death:

God of compassion,
comfort us with the great power of your love
as we mourn the sudden death of N.
In our grief and confusion,
help us find peace
in the knowledge of your loving mercy to all your
    children,
and give us light to guide us
into the assurance of your love;
through Jesus Christ our Lord.
Amen.

Silence may be observed for reflection and prayer.
The Lord's Supper may be celebrated at this point; if it is not,
    the prayers conclude with the Lord's Prayer.

Lord's Prayer

The minister invites all present to sing or say the Lord's Prayer.

And now, with the confidence of the children of God, let
us pray:

All pray together.

Or

Our Father in heaven,	**Our Father, who art in**
hallowed be your name,	**heaven,**
your kingdom come,	**hallowed be thy name,**

your will be done,
on earth as in heaven.
Give us today our daily
    bread.
Forgive us our sins
as we forgive those who
    sin against us.
Save us from the time
    of trial
and deliver us from evil.
For the kingdom, the
    power, and the glory
    are yours
now and forever. Amen.

thy kingdom come,
thy will be done,
on earth as it is in heaven.
Give us this day our daily
    bread;
and forgive us our debts,
as we forgive our debtors;
and lead us not into
    temptation,
but deliver us from evil.
For thine is the kingdom,
and the power, and the
    glory, forever. Amen.

Commendation

The people may sing a hymn, or the following may be sung:

You only are immortal, the creator and maker of all.
We are mortal, formed of the earth,
and to earth shall we return.
This you ordained when you created us, saying,
"You are dust,
and to dust you shall return."
All of us go down to the dust;
yet even at the grave we make our song:
Alleluia, alleluia, alleluia.

Give rest, O Christ, to your servant with all your saints,
where there is neither pain nor sorrow nor sighing,
but life everlasting.

The people may stand.

The minister, facing the body, says one of the following:

1

Into your hands, merciful Savior,
we commend your servant N.
Acknowledge, we humbly pray,
a sheep of your own fold,
a lamb of your own flock,
a sinner of your own redeeming.
Receive *him/her* into the arms of your mercy,
into the blessed rest of everlasting peace,
and into the glorious company of the saints in light.
Amen.

2

Holy God,
by your creative power you gave us life,
and in your redeeming love you have given us new life
    in Christ.
We commend N. to your merciful care
in the faith of Christ our Lord
who died and rose again to save us,
and who now lives and reigns with you and the
    Holy Spirit,

one God, now and forever.
Amen.

Blessing

*The minister may then pronounce God's blessing on the people,
using one of the following:*

1   *Heb. 13:20, 21*

The God of peace,
who brought back from the dead our Lord Jesus,
make you complete in everything good
so that you may do God's will,
working among us that which is pleasing in God's sight,
through Jesus Christ,
to whom be the glory forever and ever!

2   *See Phil. 4:7*

The peace of God,
which passes all understanding,
keep your hearts and minds
in the knowledge and love of God,
and of God's Son, Jesus Christ our Lord;
and the blessing of God almighty,
the Father, the Son, and the Holy Spirit,
remain with you always.
Amen.

3

May God in endless mercy,
bring the whole church,
the living and departed,
to a joyful resurrection
in the fulfillment of the eternal kingdom.
Amen.

Procession

The procession forms and leaves the church, the minister pre-
ceding the coffin. As the procession leaves the church, a
psalm, a hymn, or this canticle may be sung or said. The
pall may be removed before the coffin leaves the church and
is taken to the place of interment.

Luke 2:29-32
PH 603-605; PS 164-166

Now, Lord, you let your servant go in peace:
Your word has been fulfilled.
My own eyes have seen the salvation
which you have prepared in the sight of every people:
a light to reveal you to the nations
and the glory of your people Israel.

Glory to the Father, and to the Son,
and to the Holy Spirit,
as it was in the beginning,
is now, and will be forever. Amen.

The Committal

Outline

Scripture Sentences
Committal
Lord's Prayer
Prayers
Blessing

If preferred, the committal service may take place before the general service. In either case, the minister precedes the body (or ashes) to the appointed place, saying one or more of the following sentences:

Scripture Sentences

1   *Job 19:25*

I know that my Redeemer lives,
and that at the last he will stand upon the earth.

2   *John 11:25-26*

I am the resurrection and the life, says the Lord.
Those who believe in me, even though they die,
    shall live,
and everyone who lives and believes in me will
    never die.

3   *2 Cor. 5:1*

We know that if the earthly tent we live in is destroyed,
we have a building from God,
a house not made with hands,
eternal in the heavens.

4   *Rev. 1:17-18; John 14:19*

Do not be afraid,
I am the first and the last,
and the living one.
I was dead, and behold,
I am alive forever and ever.
Because I live, you also will live.

5   *Rom. 14:8*

If we live, we live to the Lord,
and if we die, we die to the Lord;
so then, whether we live or whether we die,
we are the Lord's.

6   *Ps. 16:11*

You show me the path of life;
in your presence there is fullness of joy;
in your right hand are pleasures forevermore.

7 *John 6:68*

Lord, to whom shall we go?
You have the words of eternal life.

8

Christ is risen from the dead,
trampling down death by death,
and giving life to those in the tomb.

When there is no other service than the committal service, a
  prayer may be said after the people have gathered.

Committal

Earth burial

The coffin is lowered into the grave or placed in its resting place.
  While earth is cast on the coffin, the minister says:

In sure and certain hope of the resurrection to
    eternal life,
through our Lord Jesus Christ,
we commend to almighty God our *brother/sister* N.,
and we commit *his/her* body to the ground,
earth to earth, ashes to ashes, dust to dust.

Rev. 14:13

Blessed are the dead who die in the Lord, says the Spirit.
They rest from their labors,
and their works follow them.

Burial at sea

As the body is lowered into the water, the minister says:

In sure and certain hope of the resurrection to eternal
    life, through our Lord Jesus Christ,
we commend to almighty God our *brother/sister* N.,
and we commit *his/her* body to the deep.

Rev. 14:13

Blessed are the dead who die in the Lord, says the Spirit.
They rest from their labors,
and their works follow them.

At a cremation service

As the body is placed in the crematory, the minister says:

In sure and certain hope of the resurrection to
    eternal life,
through our Lord Jesus Christ,
we commend to almighty God our *brother/sister* N.,
and we commit *his/her* body to be returned to
    its elements,
ashes to ashes, dust to dust.

Rev. 14:13

Blessed are the dead who die in the Lord, says the Spirit.
They rest from their labors,
and their works follow them.

At a columbarium

As the ashes are placed in their resting place, the minister says:

In sure and certain hope of the resurrection to
    eternal life,
through our Lord Jesus Christ,
we commend to almighty God our *brother/sister* N.,
and we commit *his/her* ashes to their final resting place.

Rev. 14:13

Blessed are the dead who die in the Lord, says the Spirit.
They rest from their labors,
and their works follow them.

Lord's Prayer

The Lord's Prayer may be said.

The minister says:

And now, with the confidence of the children of God,
let us pray:

All pray together:

Or

Our Father in heaven,	Our Father, who art in
hallowed be your name,	heaven,
your kingdom come,	hallowed be thy name,
your will be done,	thy kingdom come,
on earth as in heaven.	thy will be done,

Give us today our daily
  bread.
Forgive us our sins
as we forgive those who
  sin against us.
Save us from the time
  of trial
and deliver us from evil.
For the kingdom, the
  power, and the glory
  are yours
now and forever. Amen.

on earth as it is in heaven.
Give us this day our daily
  bread;
and forgive us our debts,
as we forgive our debtors;
and lead us not into
temptation,
but deliver us from evil.
For thine is the kingdom,
  and the power, and the
  glory, forever. Amen.

Prayers

*The minister says one or more of the following, or other appro-
  priate prayers.*

1

O Lord, support us all the day long
until the shadows lengthen
and the evening comes
and the busy world is hushed,
and the fever of life is over,
and our work is done.
Then, in your mercy,
grant us a safe lodging,
and a holy rest,
and peace at the last;
through Jesus Christ our Lord.
Amen.

2

O God,
you have designed this world,
and know all things good for us.
Give us such faith
that, by day and by night,
in all times and in all places,
we may without fear
entrust those who are dear to us
to your never-failing love,
in this life and in the life to come;
through Jesus Christ our Lord.
Amen.

3

God of all mercies
and giver of all comfort:
Look graciously, we pray, on those who mourn,
that, casting all their care on you,
they may know the consolation of your love;
through Jesus Christ our Lord.
Amen.

4

Almighty God,
Father of the whole family in heaven and on earth:
Stand by those who sorrow,
that, as they lean on your strength,
they may be upheld,

and believe the good news of life beyond life;
through Jesus Christ our Lord.
Amen.

5

God of boundless compassion,
our only sure comfort in distress:
Look tenderly upon your children
overwhelmed by loss and sorrow.
Lighten our darkness with your presence
and assure us of your love.
Enable us to see beyond this place and time
to your eternal kingdom,
promised to all who love you in Christ the Lord.
Amen.

6

Merciful God,
you heal the broken in heart
and bind up the wounds of the afflicted.
Strengthen us in our weakness,
calm our troubled spirits,
and dispel our doubts and fears.
In Christ's rising from the dead
you conquered death and opened the gates to
    everlasting life.
Renew our trust in you
that by the power of your love
we shall one day be brought together again
with our *brother/sister.*

Grant this, we pray, through Jesus Christ our Lord.
Amen.

7

God of all consolation,
our refuge and strength in sorrow,
by dying, our Lord Jesus Christ conquered death;
by rising from the grave he restored us to life.
Enable us to go forward in faith to meet him,
that, when our life on earth is ended,
we may be united with all who love him
in your heavenly kingdom,
where every tear will be wiped away;
through Jesus Christ our Lord.
Amen.

8

Gracious God,
your mercies are beyond number.
Lead us, by your Spirit,
in holiness and righteousness,
in confidence and a living faith,
and in the strength of a sure hope,
that we may live in favor with you,
and in perfect love with all;
through Jesus Christ our Lord.
Amen.

9

God, whose days are without end:
Help us always to remember how brief life is,
and that the hour of our death is known only to you.
Lead us, by your Holy Spirit,
to live in holiness and justice all our days.
Then after serving you in the fellowship of your church,
in faith, hope, and love,
may we enter with joy into the fullness of your
    kingdom,
through Jesus Christ our Lord.
Amen.

10

Rest eternal grant *him/her,* O Lord;
and let light perpetual shine upon *him/her.*

11

At the committal of a child

Loving God,
your beloved Son took children into his arms and
    blessed them.
Give us grace
that we may entrust N. to your never-failing care and
    love,
and bring us all to your heavenly kingdom;
through Jesus Christ our Lord.
Amen.

12

At the committal of a child

Loving God,
give us faith to believe,
though this child has died,
that you welcome *him/her*
and will care for *him/her*
until, by your mercy,
we are together again in the joy of your promised
kingdom;
through Jesus Christ osur Lord.
Amen.

Blessing

The minister dismisses the people with one of the following blessings.

1   *2 Cor. 13:14*

The grace of the Lord Jesus Christ,
the love of God,
and the communion of the Holy Spirit
be with you all.
Amen.

2   *See Num. 6:24-26*

The Lord bless you and keep you.
The Lord be kind and gracious to you.

The Lord look upon you with favor
and give you peace.
Amen.

3   *See Phil. 4:7*

The peace of God,
which passes all understanding,
keep your hearts and minds
in the knowledge and love of God,
and of God's Son, Jesus Christ our Lord;
and the blessing of God almighty,
the Father, the Son, and the Holy Spirit,
remain with you always.
Amen.

4   *Heb. 13:20-21*

Go in peace,
and may the God of peace,
who brought back from the dead our Lord Jesus,
make you complete in everything good
so that you may do God's will,
working among us that which is pleasing in God's sight,
through Jesus Christ,
to whom be the glory forever and ever!
Amen.

A UNITED CHURCH OF CHRIST SERVICE

Order of Thanksgiving for One Who Has Died

Introduction

In the Christian community, death is a corporate experience that touches the life of the entire family of faith. When a death occurs, the immediate family is encouraged to notify the church as soon as possible and to share fully in planning a service. They may also assist in leading the service. Sensitive consideration is to be given to ethnic traditions, local customs, and the particular circumstances of the bereaved.

The service recognizes both the pain and sorrow of the separation that accompanies death and the hope and joy of the promises of God to those who die and are raised in Jesus Christ. The service celebrates the life of the deceased, gives thanks for that person's life, and commends that life to God. It offers consolation to the bereaved by acknowledging their grief and anger or guilt.

It provides the Christian community and others an opportunity to support the bereaved with their presence. Its purpose is to affirm once more the powerful, steadfast love of God from which people cannot be separated, even by death.

The service is an act of corporate worship: God's word is read and proclaimed, hymns may be sung, prayers offered, and the sacrament of Holy Communion shared by those who desire it. The service should be at an hour convenient for the immediate family and the community of faith. If possible, the service most appropriately is held in the place where the congregation regularly gathers for worship. If it is held in another place, it is important that it remain a corporate act of the church's worship. This order, or some other, in the hands of the congregation will enable full participation in the service.

The presence of the coffin may help the bereaved and the congregation to confront and deal with the reality of death. The coffin is closed for the service. A white pall or another appropriate covering may be placed over the coffin symbolizing the resurrection, de-emphasizing the relative expense of coffins, and showing the equality of all people in the services of the church.

The service may also be used when the body of the deceased is not present. Then the committal service may be held prior to this service, within it, or following it.

If it is the custom of the congregation to use a large paschal candle, it is lighted as a symbol of resurrection faith. If the coffin is present, the candle is placed near the coffin.

Christians often hold membership in praiseworthy organizations other than the church. It is most appropriate for memorial rituals of those groups to be held apart from the Order for Thanksgiving for One Who Has Died to avoid compromising this service's integrity.

Customs surrounding death vary, especially those related to racial and ethnic traditions. Local churches may observe special anniversaries of a death or hold a service once a year to remember all who have died during the year. Prayers, readings, and ritual observances from various traditions may be incorporated at all remembrance times.

Outline

Prelude
Procession and Sentences
Hymn of Adoration
Greeting
Prayer
Reading of Scripture
Sermon
Words of Remembrance
Affirmation of Faith
Hymn, Anthem, or Other Music
Prayers of Thanksgiving and Intercession

Order for Holy
Communion from Brief
Order for the Service of
Word and Sacrament,
beginning with the
communion prayer

Silence
Prayer of Our Savior

Commendation
Song of Simeon
Benediction
Hymn
Postlude

Prelude

The service may begin with music for a service of the resurrection. If the coffin is set in place before the people arrive or is not present at all, the service may continue with the opening hymn or the greeting.

Procession and Sentences

If the coffin is brought into the church in a procession, a leader may meet it at the entrance and say any of the following sentences as she or he precedes the coffin and family up the aisle to the chancel. If there is no procession, the sentences may be used following the greeting. Those who are able may stand for the procession. The one presiding may say one or more sentences.

Leader
Hear the promises of God.

Leader
God is near to all who call,
who call from their hearts.
The desires of those who fear God are fulfilled;

their cries are heard;
they are saved.

B

Leader
I am the resurrection and the life;
all who believe in me,
though they die,
yet shall they live,
and whoever lives and believes in me shall never die.

C

Leader
Fear not,
I am the first and the last,
and the living one;
I died, and behold I am alive for evermore.

D

Leader
Fear not,
for I am with you,
be not dismayed,
for I am your God;
I will strengthen you,
I will help you,
I will uphold you with my victorious hand.

Leader
When we were baptized into Christ Jesus,
we were baptized into Christ's death.
By our baptism, then,
we were buried with Christ,
and shared Christ's death,
in order that,
just as Christ was raised from death
by the glorious power of God,
so too we might live a new life.
For if we have been united with Christ
in a death like Christ's,
we shall certainly be united with Christ
in a resurrection like Christ's.

Leader
Blessed are the dead
who die in Christ.
"Blessed indeed," says the Spirit,
"that they may rest from their labors,
for their deeds follow them!"

Hymn of Adoration

*As the procession nears the chancel, a hymn may be sung. If
there is no procession, the people who are able may rise for
the opening hymn as a leader enters; or a leader may enter
during the prelude and open with the greeting and/or the
sentences. Then the service may continue with the hymn.*

Greeting

*All who are able may stand. A leader may greet the people
informally, name the person for whom they gather in
thanksgiving, and interpret briefly the meaning of the service. One or more of the following greetings may be used.*

Leader
The grace of our Lord Jesus Christ
and the love of God
and the communion of the Holy Spirit
be with you all.

People
And also with you.

Leader
Friends,
we gather here in the protective shelter
of God's healing love.
We are free to pour out our grief,
release our anger,
face our emptiness,
and know that God cares.
We gather here as God's people,
conscious of others who have died
and of the frailty
of our own existence on earth.
We come to comfort and to support one another

in our common loss.
We gather to hear God's word of hope
that can drive away our despair
and move us to offer God our praise.
We gather to commend to God with thanksgiving
the life of _____

name

as we celebrate the good news of Christ's resurrection.
For whether we live or whether we die,
we belong to Christ who is Lord
both of the dead and of the living.

C

Leader
Gracious is our God and righteous;
our God is full of compassion.
People
I will walk in the presence of God
in the land of the living.
Leader
I will fulfill my vows to God
in the presence of all God's people.
People
Precious in the sight of God
is the death of those who die in faithfulness.

Prayer

The people may be seated. The service may continue with a
confession of sin and an assurance of pardon or a collect or
a prayer of thanksgiving for the communion of saints.

A

Leader
The peace of Christ
be with you.
People
And also with you.
Leader
Let us pray.
All
Almighty God,
whose will is sovereign
and whose mercy is
boundless, look upon
us in our sorrow and
enable us to hear
your word.
Help us hear so that,
through patience
and the encouragement
of the scriptures,
we may hold fast to the
assurance of your favor
and the hope of life
eternal; through
Jesus Christ our
risen Savior.
Amen.

B

All
Holy God,
whose ways are not our
ways and whose thoughts
are not our thoughts,
grant that your Holy
Spirit may intercede
for us with sighs
too deep for human
words. Heal our
wounded hearts made
heavy by our sorrow.
Through the veil of
our tears and the
silence of our
emptiness, assure us
again that ear has
not heard, nor eye
seen, nor human
imagination
envisioned,
what you have
prepared for those
who love you;
through Jesus Christ,
the first-born from
the dead.
Amen.

Reading of Scripture

The psalms, read responsively or antiphonally or sung, may be used before and/or after the lessons. It is appropriate to include at least one Gospel lesson. Where it is the custom, all who are able may stand for the Gospel reading. Members of the family of the deceased and other lay persons may be readers. A gloria may be said or sung at the conclusion of the final psalm. Suggested readings include the following.

Psalms

Psalms 23; 27:7-14; 42:1-5; 46; 90:1-4, 12-17; 121; 130; 139:1-18, 23-24

Old Testament

Job 19:25-27; Isaiah 25:6-9; 61:1-3; Lamentations 3:22-26, 31-33

Epistles

Acts 10:34-43
Romans 8:9-11, 31-39
1 Corinthians 13; 15:12-20; 15:35-50
2 Corinthians 4:7-11, 16; 5:1-5
Ephesians 3:14-21
1 Thessalonians 4:13-18
2 Timothy 1:8-13
Revelation 21:1-6

Gospels

Matthew 5:3-10; 11:28-30

Luke 23:33, 39-43
John 6:37-40; 11:17-27; 12:24-26; 14:1-3, 18-19, 25-27

Sermon

The people may be seated for a sermon.

Words of Remembrance

*A leader or a friend or member of the family of the deceased
may offer thanksgiving for the one who has died and recall
the individual uniqueness if this is desired and has not been
done during the sermon.*

Affirmation of Faith

*All who are able may stand and affirm the resurrection faith
by saying a creed, statement of faith, or other affirmation,
such as the following from Romans.*

Leader
Let us say again what we believe.

All
We believe there is no condemnation
for those who are in Christ Jesus,
and we know that in everything
God works for good with those who love God,
who are called according to God's purpose.
We are sure that neither death, nor life,
nor angels, nor principalities,
nor things present, nor things to come,

132

nor powers, nor height, nor depth,
nor anything else in all creation,
will be able to separate us
from the love of God in Christ Jesus our Lord.
Amen.

Hymn, Anthem, or Other Music

Music may be offered in God's praise.

Prayers of Thanksgiving and Intercession

These or other similar prayers may be offered. A litany may be
used. The prayers may be used individually or together, with
or without each "Amen" said by the pastor or people. Prayers
to be offered at the death of a child follow the general prayers.

Leader
Let us pray.

A

Leader
Merciful God, we thank you for your word;
it is a lamp for our feet, a light for our path.
We thank you especially that in the night of our grief
and the shadows of our sorrow,
we are not left to ourselves.
We have the light of your promises
to sustain and comfort us.
Through our tears,
give us vision to see in faith

the consolation you intend for us.
In your mercy,
grant us the unfailing guidance of your saving Word,
both in life and in death;
through Jesus Christ our risen Savior.

People
Amen.

B

Leader
O God, our strength and our redeemer,
giver of life and conqueror of death,
we praise you with humble hearts.
With faith in your great mercy and wisdom,
we entrust _____ to your eternal care.
                    name

We praise you for your steadfast love for *her/him* all
the days of *her/his* earthly life.

We thank you for all that *he/she* was
to those who loved *him/her*
and for *his/her* faithfulness
to the church of Jesus Christ.

Mention may be made of the person's Christian life and service.

We thank you that for _____
                              name

all sickness and sorrow are ended, and
death itself is past

134

and that *she/he* has entered the home
where all your people gather in peace.
Keep us all in communion with your faithful people
in every time and place,
that at last we may rejoice together in the heavenly
    family
where Jesus Christ reigns
with you and the Holy Spirit,
one God, for ever.

People
Amen.

Leader
God of all mercies and all comfort,
in tender love and compassion,
embrace your sorrowing servants.
Be their refuge and strength,
an ever present help in trouble.
Show them again the love of Christ
that passes all human understanding;
for by death Christ has conquered death,
and by rising Christ has opened to all of us
the gates of everlasting life.
Thanks be to you, O God.

People
Amen.

Leader
Let us pray for ourselves.

People
O God, whose days are without end
and whose mercies cannot be counted,
awaken us to the shortness and uncertainty of human
    life.
By your Holy Spirit,
lead us in faithfulness all our days.
When we have served you in our generation,
may we be gathered with those who have gone before,
having the testimony of a good conscience,
in the communion of your holy church,
in the confidence of a certain faith,
in the comfort of a saving hope,
in favor with you, our God,
and at perfect peace with the world;
through Jesus Christ our Redeemer.
Amen.

*At the death of a child, the following prayers or others in the
    leader's own words may be offered.*

E

Leader
**Gentle God,
born an infant in Jesus Christ
in the family of Joseph and Mary,**

136

we give you thanks for _____ born
name

among us full of hope and promise.
We remember that Jesus Christ lifted children
into loving arms to embrace and bless them.
We ask you to embrace and bless _____
name

as part of your heavenly family where,
by your grace, our lives are brought to fullness
in the peace of your eternal home.
We ask this through Jesus Christ,
your beloved child, and our risen Savior.

People
Amen.

| F | *for parents*

Leader
God of all mercies,
whose heart aches with our human hurting,
we commend to your love the parent(s) of this child,

_____,
name(s) of parent(s)

and all *his/her/their* children who mourn.

Sustain the family
in this loss and in their loneliness.
Kindle anew the ashes of joy.
Grant the peace of knowing
that this child is with you,
the Mother and Father of us all,

both in this life
and in the life that is to come;
through Jesus Christ our Savior.

People
Amen.

*If Holy Communion is not to be celebrated, the service may be
concluded with silence, the Prayer of Our Savior, the commendation, and the closing acts that follow.*

*If Holy Communion is to be celebrated, the service continues with
the offertory of the bread and wine in the Brief Order for the
Service of Word and Sacrament. Members of the family or
friends of the deceased may bring the bread and wine to the
table. All Christians present may be invited to receive.*

Silence

Silence may be observed for reflection and prayer.

Prayer of Our Savior

*Standing, sitting, or kneeling, all may sing or say the prayer
received from Jesus Christ.*

Leader
Let us pray as Christ our Savior has taught us.

A	B	C
All	*All*	*All*
Our Father in heaven, hallowed be your name, your kingdom come, your will be done, on earth as in heaven. Give us today our daily bread. Forgive us our sins as we forgive those who sin against us. Save us from the time of trial and deliver us from evil. For the kingdom, and power, and the glory are yours now and for ever. Amen.	Our Father who art in heaven, hallowed be thy name. Thy kingdom come. Thy will be done on earth as it is in heaven. Give us this day our daily bread. And forgive us our trespasses, as we forgive those who trespass against us. And lead us not into temptation, but deliver us from evil. For thine is the kingdom, and the power, and the glory for ever and ever. Amen.	Our Father who art in heaven, hallowed be thy name. Thy kingdom come. Thy will be done on earth as it is in heaven. Give us this day our daily bread. And forgive us our debts, as we forgive our debtors. And lead us not into temptation, but deliver us from evil. For thine is the kingdom, and the power, and the glory for ever. Amen.

Commendation

All who are able may stand. The leader may go to the coffin for one of the following or another commendation. The words are also appropriate if no coffin is present.

A

Leader
Holy God,
by your mighty power
you gave us life,
and in your love
you have given us new life
in Jesus Christ.
We now entrust

_____
name

to your merciful care.
We do this in the faith
of Christ Jesus,
who died and rose again
to save us and is now alive
and reigns with you
and the Holy Spirit
in glory for ever.

People
Amen.

B

Leader
Into your hands,
O merciful Savior,
we commend your servant

_____ .
name

Acknowledge,
we humbly pray,
a sheep of your own fold,
a lamb of your own flock,
and a *daughter/son*
of your own redeeming.
Receive *her/him* into the
arms of your mercy,
into the blessed rest
of everlasting peace,
and into the company
of the saints in light.

People
Amen.

Song of Simeon

All who are able may stand and sing or say the ancient Nunc Dimittis.

All
Holy One,
now let your servant go in peace;
your word has been fulfilled;
my own eyes have seen the salvation
which you have prepared in the sight of every people;
a light to reveal you to the nations
and the glory of your people Israel.

At the request of the family of the deceased or in the case of cremation, the Order for Committal may take place.

Benediction

While all who are able stand, a leader may give the benediction. According to local custom, the hymn may precede the benediction.

A	B
Leader	*Leader*
Now may the God of peace who brought again from the dead our Savior Jesus, the	May God bless you and keep you.
	People
	Amen.

great shepherd of the
sheep, by the blood
of the eternal covenant,
equip you
with everything good
that you may do God's
will, working in you that
which is pleasing in
God's sight, through
Jesus Christ; to whom
be glory for ever
and ever.

People
Amen.

Leader
May God's face shine
upon you and be
gracious to you.
People
Amen.
Leader
May God look upon you
with kindness and give
you peace.
People
Amen.

*for use, except during
Lent*

Leader
**Alleluia. Christ is
risen.**
People
Christ is risen indeed.
Alleluia.
Leader
**Let us go forth in
the name of Christ.**
People
Thanks be to God.

Hymn

All who are able may stand for a hymn. If there is to be a recessional, the leader(s) may precede the coffin and the family to the door.

Postlude

11

A BAPTIST SERVICE

Call to Worship

We gather today because the bell has tolled. Death in its untimely way has come to dwell among us.

We gather to put our arms around one another, and especially around this family, and to say to each member: you matter to us; your grief has reached into our lives, and we are sad for ourselves and for you.

We gather with broken hearts to do our grief work to the end that we might discover both comfort and courage.

And we gather to celebrate the life of (*name*), to remember the life that he lived, and to hold it before us today as one utterly unique and significant human life.

We gather, too, to worship the living God — the one who is Lord of life and of death, the Father of our Lord Jesus Christ.

Choral Introit

"Almighty God of Our Fathers"

This service was composed by and used with the permission of the Reverend Deryl Fleming while he was pastor of Ravensworth Baptist Church, Annandale, Virginia.

Invocation

Father, we stand before the mystery of life and death; help us to do it with dignity and with honesty. We celebrate the gift of life; help us to be grateful. We wait to hear from you; help us to receive your presence, through Jesus Christ our Lord, in whose name we worship and pray. **Amen.**

Introduction to the Hymn

Christian faith does not have all the answers to the mysteries of life. It does know and have the questions. It has a clue and a promise. It has a commitment and a song. Today we need to sing that song of faith in God. Will you dare to worship as we sing the hymn?

Hymn

"A Mighty Fortress"

Responsive Reading

John 13:34-35; Eph. 4:31–5:2; I John 3:14-18; 4:7

Gloria Patri

Witness to a Life

(personal eulogy)

Prayer

Anthem

"Eternal Life"

Sermon

Hymn

"O God Our Help in Ages Past"

Benediction

Almighty God, our Father, we worship thee and give thanks for the gift of life, and we dare to receive again our own lives as a gift. Grant to us the courage to live with integrity and with honesty, knowing that the meaning of life is to give our lives for the sake of our brothers. Grant to us the benediction of your grace, mercy, and peace as we go from this place to live our lives; through Jesus Christ, our Lord. **Amen.**

Postlude

"Hallelujah Chorus" from *The Messiah*

Graveside

When (*name*) walked in, the music came on. Wherever he was — at home, in church, at work, with friends — he brought music. I do not know much about heaven, but it must be filled with music today. And our lives are enhanced because of the music of his life. We know better how to sing because he lived among us. There is music in our lives because he made music in them. Not all the notes are lilting — today there are discords and silences. But one day again we will make music with our lives because of the music of (*name*)'s life.

Scripture

Rom. 8:31-32, 35, 37-39; Rev. 21:1-7

Prayer

Lord God, our Father, we commit our brother, husband, father, son, son-in-law, friend, fellow-worker, unto thee, in whose hands he already is. We are grateful that you gave him to us. We give thanks for his life, for the warm and vivid memories he left us and for the many gifts he gave us. Each of us has his or her own gratitude and his or her own grief. Give us the courage to mourn as we must and to trust thy grace to lead us out of the valley of the shadow of death, until the day when we can reaffirm life and live with keener sensitivity and deeper gratitude because of (*name*)'s life, and because of the life, death, and resurrection of our Lord Jesus Christ, in whose name we pray. **Amen.**

Benediction

The Lord bless you and keep you and make his face to shine upon you. The Lord be gracious unto you and give you peace, now and evermore. **Amen.**

12

A LUTHERAN SERVICE

Burial of the Dead

*This rite may be used as a memorial service by omitting those
portions indicated by the line in the left margin.*

*The ceremonies or tributes of social or fraternal societies have
no place within the service of the Church.*

At the Entrance to the Church

*The ministers meet the coffin, the pallbearers, and the bereaved
at the entrance to the church.*

Pastor: Blessed be the God and Father of our Lord Jesus
Christ, the source of all mercy and the God of all consolation. He comforts us in all our sorrows so that we can
comfort others in their sorrows with the consolation we
ourselves have received from God. **Thanks be to God.**

*A pall may be placed upon the coffin by the pallbearers or other
assisting ministers, and the following may be said.*

———————

The Service for Burial of the Dead is reprinted from *Lutheran Book
of Worship,* copyright 1978, by permission of Augsburg Publishing
House.

Pastor: When we were baptized in Christ Jesus, we were baptized into his death. We were buried therefore with him by baptism into death, so that as Christ was raised from the dead by the glory of the Father, we too might live a new life. For if we have been united with him in a death like his, we shall certainly be united with him in a resurrection like his.

Procession

Stand

The procession forms and enters the church, the ministers preceding the coffin.

A psalm, hymn, or appropriate verse may be sung as the procession goes to the front of the church.

The Liturgy of the Word

Pastor: The Lord be with you.
Congregation: **And also with you.**
Pastor: Let us pray.

One of the following prayers is said.

Pastor: O God of grace and glory, we remember before you today our *brother/sister, (name)*. We thank you for giving *him/her* to us to know and to love as a companion in our pilgrimage on earth. In your boundless compassion, console us who mourn. Give us your aid, so we may see in death the gate to eternal life, that we may continue our course on earth in confidence until, by your call, we are reunited with those who have gone before us; through your Son, Jesus Christ our Lord. **Amen.**

or

Pastor: Almighty God, source of all mercy and giver of comfort: Deal graciously, we pray, with those who mourn, that, casting all their sorrow on you, they may know the consolation of your love; through your Son, Jesus Christ our Lord. **Amen.**

or

Pastor: Almighty God, those who die in the Lord still live with you in joy and blessedness. We give you heartfelt thanks for the grace you have bestowed upon your servants who have finished their course in faith and now rest from their labors. May we, with all who have died in the true faith, have perfect fulfillment and joy in your eternal and everlasting glory; through your Son, Jesus Christ our Lord. **Amen.**

or

Pastor: O God, your days are without end and your mercies cannot be counted. Make us aware of the shortness and uncertainty of human life, and let your Holy Spirit lead us in holiness and righteousness all the days of our life, so that, when we shall have served you in our generation, we may be gathered to our ancestors, having the testimony of a good conscience, in the communion of your Church, in the confidence of a certain faith, in the comfort of a holy hope, in favor with you, our God, and in peace with all humanity; through Jesus Christ our Lord. **Amen.**

or

At the Burial of a Child

Pastor: O God our Father, your beloved Son took children into his arms and blessed them. Give us grace, we pray, that we may entrust (*name*) to your never-failing care and love, and bring us all to your heavenly kingdom; through your Son, Jesus Christ our Lord. **Amen.**

Sit

One or two LESSONS are read. A psalm, hymn, or anthem may be sung between the first and second readings. The appropriate VERSE may be sung:

Congregation: **Alleluia. Jesus Christ is the firstborn of the dead; to him be glory and power forever and ever. Amen. Alleluia.**

or

Lent

Congregation: **If we have died with Christ, we shall also live with him; if we are faithful to the end, we shall reign with him.**

Stand

The GOSPEL is read.

Sit

The SERMON follows the reading of the Gospel.

Stand

A HYMN is sung.
The CREED may be said.

Pastor: God has made us his people through our Baptism into Christ. Living together in trust and hope, we confess our faith.

Congregation: I believe in God, the Father almighty, creator of heaven and earth.

I believe in Jesus Christ, his only Son, our Lord.
    He was conceived by the power of the Holy Spirit
        and born of the virgin Mary.
    He suffered under Pontius Pilate,
        was crucified, died, and was buried.
    He descended into hell.*
    On the third day he rose again.
    He ascended into heaven,
        and is seated at the right hand of the Father.
    He will come again to judge the living and the dead.

I believe in the Holy Spirit,
    the holy catholic Church,
    the communion of saints,
    the forgiveness of sins,
    the resurrection of the body,
    and the life everlasting. Amen.

*Or, he descended to the dead.

Prayers

Minister: Let us pray.

Almighty God, you have knit your chosen people together in one communion, in the mystical body of your Son, Jesus Christ our Lord. Give to your whole Church in heaven and on earth your light and your peace.
Hear us, Lord.

Minister: Grant that all who have been baptized into Christ's death and resurrection may die to sin and rise to newness of life and that through the grave and gate of death we may pass with him to our joyful resurrection.
Hear us, Lord.

Minister: Grant to us who are still in our pilgrimage, and who walk as yet by faith, that your Holy Spirit may lead us in holiness and righteousness all our days.
Hear us, Lord.

Minister: Grant to your faithful people pardon and peace, that we may be cleansed from all our sins and serve you with a quiet mind.
Hear us, Lord.

Minister: Grant to all who mourn a sure confidence in your loving care, that, casting all their sorrow on you, they may know the consolation of your love.
Hear us, Lord.

Minister: Give courage and faith to those who are bereaved, that they may have strength to meet the days ahead in the comfort of a holy and certain hope, and in the joyful expectation of eternal life with those they love. **Hear us, Lord.**

Minister: Help us, we pray, in the midst of things we cannot understand, to believe and trust in the communion of saints, the forgiveness of sins, and the resurrection to life everlasting.
Hear us, Lord.

Minister: Grant us grace to entrust (*name*) to your never-failing love which sustained *him/her* in this life. Receive *him/her* into the arms of your mercy, and remember *him/her* according to the favor you bear for your people.
Hear us, Lord.

The minister concludes the intercessions with one of the following prayers.

God of all grace, you sent your Son, our Savior Jesus Christ, to bring life and immortality to light. We give thanks because by his death Jesus destroyed the power of death and by his resurrection has opened the kingdom of heaven to all believers. Make us certain that because he lives we shall live also, and that neither death nor life, nor things present nor things to come shall be able to separate us from your love which is in Christ Jesus our Lord, who lives and reigns with you and the Holy Spirit, one God, now and forever. **Amen.**

or

God, the generations rise and pass away before you. You are the strength of those who labor; you are the rest of the blessed dead. We rejoice in the company of your saints. We remember all who have lived in faith, all who have peacefully died, and especially those most dear to us who rest in you. . . . Give us in time our portion with those who have trusted in you and have striven to do your holy will. To your name, with the Church on earth and the Church in heaven, we ascribe all honor and glory, now and forever. **Amen.**

When Holy Communion is celebrated, the service continues with the Peace. The Commendation then follows the post-communion canticle ("Lord, now you let your servant . . .") and prayer.

When there is no Communion, the service continues with the Lord's Prayer:

Our Father in heaven,
    hallowed be your name,
    your kingdom come,
    your will be done,
        on earth as in heaven.
Give us today our daily bread.
Forgive us our sins
as we forgive those
        who sin against us.
Save us from the time of trial
    and deliver us from evil.
For the kingdom, the power

and the glory are yours
    now and forever. Amen.

or

Our Father, who art in heaven,
    hallowed be thy name,
    thy kingdom come;
    thy will be done,
        on earth as it is in heaven.
Give us this day our daily bread;
and forgive us our trespasses,
    as we forgive those
        who trespass against us;
and lead us not into temptation,
    but deliver us from evil.
For thine is the kingdom,
    and the power, and the glory,
        forever and ever. Amen.

Sit

Commendation

The ministers take their places at the coffin.

Pastor: Into your hands, O merciful Savior, we commend your servant, (*name*). Acknowledge, we humbly beseech you, a sheep of your own fold, a lamb of your own flock, a sinner of your own redeeming. Receive *him/her* into the arms of your mercy, into the blessed rest of everlasting peace, and into the glorious company of the saints in light. **Amen.**

Pastor: Let us go forth in peace.
In the name of Christ. Amen.

Stand
The procession forms and leaves the church, the ministers preceding the coffin.
As the procession leaves the church, a psalm, hymn, or anthem may be sung. The canticle, "Lord, now you let your servant . . . ," may be sung if it has not been sung in the Holy Communion.

Committal

The ministers precede the coffin to the place of interment. During the procession, one or more of these verses may be sung or said.

Minister: I called to the Lord in my distress; the Lord answered by setting me free. It is better to rely on the Lord than to put any trust in flesh. It is better to rely on the Lord than to put any trust in rulers.

I was pressed so hard that I almost fell, but the Lord came to my help.

There is a sound of exultation and victory in the tents of the righteous:

"The right hand of the Lord has triumphed! The right hand of the Lord is exalted! The right hand of the Lord has triumphed!"

I shall not die, but live, and declare the works of the Lord.

Open for me the gates of righteousness; I will enter them; I will offer thanks to the Lord. "This is the gate of the Lord; he who is righteous may enter." (Ps. 118:5, 8-9, 13, 15-17, 19-20)

Minister: For I know that my Redeemer lives, and at last he will stand upon the earth; and after my skin has been thus destroyed, then from my flesh I shall see God. (Job 19:25-26)

Minister: None of us lives to himself, and none of us dies to himself. If we live, we live to the Lord, and if we die, we die to the Lord; for then, whether we live or whether we die, we are the Lord's. (Rom. 14:7-8)

Minister: "I am the resurrection and the life," says the Lord; "he who believes in me, though he die, yet shall he live, and whoever lives and believes in me shall never die." (John 11:25-26*a*)

When all have arrived at the place of burial, the following prayer may be said.

Pastor: Almighty God, by the death and burial of Jesus, your anointed, you have destroyed death and sanctified the graves of all your saints. Keep our *brother/sister* whose *body* we now lay to rest, in the company of all your saints, and at the last, raise *him/her* up to share with all your faithful people the endless joy and peace won through the glorious resurrection of Christ our Lord, who lives and reigns with you and the Holy Spirit, one God, now and forever. **Amen.**

One of the following lessons may be read.

And Jesus answered them, "The hour has come for the son of man to be glorified. Truly, truly, I say to you, unless a grain of wheat falls into the earth and dies, it remains alone; but if it dies, it bears much fruit. He who loves his life loses it, and he who hates his life in this world will keep it for eternal life. If anyone serves me, he must follow me; and where I am, there shall my servant be also; if anyone serves me, the Father will honor him." (John 12:23-26)

Lo! I tell you a mystery. We shall not all sleep, but we shall all be changed, in a moment, in the twinkling of an eye, at the last trumpet. For the trumpet will sound, and the dead will be raised imperishable, and we shall be changed. For this perishable nature must put on the imperishable, and this mortal nature must put on immortality. When the perishable puts on the imperishable, and the mortal puts on immortality, then shall come to pass the saying that is written: "Death is swallowed up in victory." "O death, where is thy victory? O death, where is thy sting?" The sting of death is sin, and the power of sin is the law. But thanks be to God, who gives us the victory through our Lord Jesus Christ. (I Cor. 15:51-57)

But our commonwealth is in heaven, and from it we await a Savior, the Lord Jesus Christ, who will change our lowly body to be like his glorious body, by the power which enables him even to subject all things to himself. (Phil. 3:20-21)

The coffin is lowered into the grave or placed in its resting place.
Earth may be cast on the coffin as the minister says:

159

In sure and certain hope of the resurrection to eternal life through our Lord Jesus Christ, we commend to almighty God our *brother/sister,* (*name*), and we commit *his/her* body to *the ground/the deep/the elements/its resting place;* earth to earth, ashes to ashes, dust to dust. The Lord bless *him/her* and keep *him/her.* The Lord make his face shine on *him/her* and be gracious to *him/her.* The Lord look upon *him/her* with favor and give *him/her* peace. **Amen.**

or

Since almighty God has called our *brother/sister,* (*name*), from this life to himself, we commit *his/her* body to *the earth from which it was made/the deep/the elements/its resting place.* Christ was the first to rise from the dead, and we know that he will raise up our mortal bodies to be like his in glory. We commend our *brother/sister* to the Lord: May the Lord receive *him/her* into his peace and raise *him/her* up on the last day. **Amen.**

Pastor: Lord, remember us in your kingdom, and teach us to pray:

Our Father in heaven,
    hallowed be your name,
    your kingdom come,
    your will be done,
        on earth as in heaven.
Give us today our daily bread.
Forgive us our sins
    as we forgive those
        who sin against us.
Save us from the time of trial

and deliver us from evil.
For the kingdom, the power,
and the glory are yours
now and forever. Amen.

or

Our Father, who art in heaven,
hallowed be thy name,
thy kingdom come,
thy will be done,
on earth as it is in heaven.
Give us this day our daily bread;
and forgive us our trespasses
as we forgive those
who trespass against us;
and lead us not into temptation,
but deliver us from evil.
For thine is the kingdom,
and the power, and the glory,
forever and ever. Amen.

Pastor: Lord Jesus, by your death you took away the sting of death. Grant to us, your servants, so to follow in faith where you have led the way, that we may at length fall asleep peacefully in you and wake in your likeness; to you, the author and giver of life, be all honor and glory, now and forever. **Amen.**

Then may be said:

Pastor: Rest eternal grant *him/her*
Minister: And let light perpetual shine upon *him/her.*

The minister blesses the people:
The God of peace — who brought again from the dead our Lord Jesus Christ, the great shepherd of the sheep, through the blood of the everlasting covenant — make you perfect in every good work to do his will, working in you that which is well-pleasing in his sight; through Jesus Christ, to whom be glory forever and ever. **Amen.**

Pastor: Let us go in peace.

13

SERVICE FOR THE BURIAL OF A CHILD

*For use at the church, house, or funeral home. The coffin should
be closed before the service begins and remain closed. One or
more of the following sentences may be said by the minister.*

Jesus said, "Let the children come to me, do not hinder them;
for to such belongs the kingdom of God." (Mark 10:14)

Wait for the Lord; be strong, and let your heart take
courage; yea, wait for the Lord. (Ps. 27:14)

He will feed his flock like a shepherd, he will gather the lambs
in his arms, he will carry them in his bosom. (Isa. 40:11)

As a father pities his children, so the Lord pities those who
fear him. (Ps. 103:13)

Blessed are those who mourn, for they shall be comforted.
(Matt. 5:4)

As one whom his mother comforts, so I will comfort you,
says the Lord. (Isa. 66:13)

This service was composed by Perry H. Biddle, Jr.

The eternal God is your dwelling place, and underneath are the everlasting arms. (Deut. 33:27)

Prayer

Our loving heavenly Father, who hears us while we are yet calling to you, whose ear is ever open to the cry of your children, and who has been and is a very present help in time of trouble, we turn to you in this hour of sorrow. We know your abiding love for us in Christ Jesus our Lord. Trusting in your perfect wisdom and steadfast mercy, we seek your comforting presence; through Jesus Christ our Redeemer. **Amen.**

Psalm 23 may be said or sung by the congregation. Two or more of the following lessons shall be read, concluding with one from the Gospels.

Who shall separate us from the love of Christ? Shall tribulation, or distress, or persecution, or famine, or nakedness, or peril, or sword? . . . No, in all these things we are more than conquerors through him who loved us. For I am sure that neither death, nor life, nor angels, nor principalities, nor things present, nor things to come, nor powers, nor height, nor depth, nor anything else in all creation, will be able to separate us from the love of God in Christ Jesus our Lord. (Rom. 8:35, 37-39)

At that time the disciples came to Jesus, saying, "Who is the greatest in the kingdom of heaven?" And calling to him a child, he put him in the midst of them, and said, "Truly, I say to you, unless you turn and become like children, you will never enter the kingdom of heaven. Whoever humbles himself like this child, he is the greatest in the kingdom of heaven.

"Whoever receives one such child in my name receives me. . . .

"See that you do not despise one of these little ones; for I tell you that in heaven their angels always behold the face of my Father who is in heaven. What do you think? If a man has a hundred sheep, and one of them has gone astray, does he not leave the ninety-nine on the mountains and go in search of the one that went astray? And if he finds it, truly, I say to you, he rejoices over it more than over the ninety-nine that never went astray. So it is not the will of my Father who is in heaven that one of these little ones should perish." (Matt. 18:1-5, 10-14)

They were bringing children to Jesus, that he might touch them; and the disciples rebuked them. But when Jesus saw it he was indignant, and said to them, "Let the children come to me, do not hinder them; for to such belongs the kingdom of God. Truly, I say to you, whoever does not receive the kingdom of God like a child shall not enter it." And he took them in his arms and blessed them, laying his hands upon them. (Mark 10:13-16)

Jesus said, "Let not your hearts be troubled; believe in God, believe also in me. In my Father's house are many rooms; if it were not so, would I have told you that I go to prepare a place for you? And when I go and prepare a place for you, I will come again and will take you to myself, that where I am you may be also. And you know the way where I am going." Thomas said to him, "Lord, we do not know where you are going; how can we know the way?"

Jesus said to him, "I am the way, and the truth, and the life; no one comes to the Father, but by me. . . .

"I will not leave you desolate; I will come to you. Yet a little while, and the world will see me no more, but you will see me; because I live, you will live also. . . .

"Peace I leave with you; my peace I give to you; not as the world gives do I give to you. Let not your hearts be troubled, neither let them be afraid." (John 14:1-6, 18-19, 27)

Here a sermon may be preached witnessing to the resurrection and offering the strong comfort of God.
Prayers of thanksgiving and intercession shall be offered.

Almighty God, who loves each of us as if we were the only one you have to love and yet who loves us all the same, we thank you for creating humans in your image. We praise and thank you that you gave your only Son Jesus Christ to take our nature upon himself, to suffer death upon the cross for our redemption and to rise victorious over sin and death. With all the heavenly host we join in praising and magnifying your gracious name, saying:

> Holy, holy, holy Lord God of hosts;
>   heaven and earth are full of your glory.
> Glory be to you, O Lord most high.

Our Father, we remember how your Son Jesus Christ took little children into his arms and blessed them. We thank you that you gave this child to us and moved our hearts to love him (her) and your church to cherish him (her). We praise and bless you for the assurance that you have received him (her) to yourself to keep now and always in the arms of your mercy; through Jesus Christ our Lord. **Amen.**

Let us pray for those who mourn.

O God, unto whom all hearts are open, all desires known, and from whom no secrets are hidden, you know the needs of each of us as we grieve. Your compassion never fails. Give to those who mourn your strength and consolation so that they may be upheld by a living hope. Let them hear the words of your Son our Savior which reveal his love for little children and speak peace to their troubled hearts. Assure them that the child who has been taken out of their sight is with you, safe in your eternal care, and that in your own good time they will see him (her) again; through Jesus Christ our Lord. **Amen.**

The congregation joins the minister in the Lord's Prayer.
A hymn may be sung.
The blessing by the minister:

The Lord bless you and keep you. The Lord make his face to shine upon you and be gracious to you. The Lord lift up his countenance upon you and give you peace. In the name of the Father, and of the Son, and of the Holy Spirit. **Amen.**

When only a graveside service is held, the above service may be
  abbreviated and combined with the following.

The Committal Service

One or more of these sentences may be used:

The eternal God is your dwelling place, and underneath are the everlasting arms. (Deut. 33:27)

Jesus said, "Let the children come to me, do not hinder them; for to such belongs the kingdom of God." (Mark 10:14)

As a father pities his children, so the Lord pities those who fear him. (Ps. 103:13)

As one whom his mother comforts, so I will comfort you, says the Lord. (Isa. 66:13)

Then shall be said the words of committal:

Trusting in our Lord Jesus Christ, who took little children in his arms and blessed them, we commit to the ground the body of this child in the assurance that he (she) lives in the glory of God's presence and that he (she) is safe in his arms for evermore.

At a cremation or entombment appropriate words may be substituted.

Prayer of intercession:

Our loving heavenly Father, who loves all that you have made, comfort your servants in their great sorrow. Give to them a greater measure of your tender mercies. May they so love and serve you in this life that together with this your child they may obtain the fullness of your promises in the world to come. Through Jesus Christ our Lord. **Amen.**

The blessing:

Now may the God of peace, who brought again from the dead our Lord Jesus, the great Shepherd of the sheep, through the blood of the everlasting covenant, equip you with everything good so that you may do his will, working in you that which is pleasing in his sight; through Jesus Christ, to whom be glory for ever and ever. **Amen.**

14

A FREE SERVICE

A MEMORIAL SERVICE

Mary Esther Hickman was killed at the age of sixteen while with her family on vacation in Colorado. Mary's body was cremated.

When the family returned to their home in Nashville, a memorial service was held at Edgehill United Methodist Church. In the chancel area and at the door were several large pictures of Mary, flowers, and several significant objects relating to Mary — a poster that had hung in her room, a Mexican God's-eye yarn hanging which she had requested for her seventeenth birthday (August 4; the memorial service was on August 1), a butterfly-shaped geode which she had bought the day before her death for her great-grandmother's ninety-eighth birthday, and a memorial candle which the family had bought after her death and used at the Colorado service. The family was seated in the front row of the congregation.

Music significant for the family, including "Bridge over Troubled Water," was played on the piano as a prelude.

Written by and used by permission of the Reverend Hoyt Hickman, father of Mary Hickman.

The congregation stood, the pastor spoke sentences of hope and comfort from the Scriptures and read the Twenty-third Psalm. He then prayed, and the congregation prayed the Lord's Prayer in unison. The congregation sang "Precious Lord."

The youth minister, who was a good friend of Mary, read portions of the eighth chapter of Romans and preached on the text "The Spirit himself intercedes for us with sighs too deep for words."

Another of Mary's friends, the counselor of her church youth group, accompanying himself on the guitar, sang "One Day at a Time," which well expressed Mary's approach to life.

Those present were invited to share with one another as the Spirit moved them. Mary's high school English teacher spoke of Mary and read from her writings. One of her brothers read a poem she had written. Her father and mother, referring to the objects in the room and recent conversations with Mary, expressed their Christian grief and hope, and their need for the community of love. Friends, both youths and adults, shared their faith and love.

The congregation sang "Joy Is Like the Rain."

The people were invited to come forward and stand with the family around the Lord's Table for Holy Communion. The associate minister took the bread and the cup, gave thanks, broke the bread — a loaf baked by a friend — and gave the bread and the cup to the people, who served one another, hand to hand. They sang "Amazing Grace" with dulcimer accompaniment, received the benediction, then sang "Shalom" — the congregation's customary closing song. The people spontaneously shared their love with the family while still standing together and then gradually dispersed.

At a later time, Mary's ashes were buried in the family plot at Holyoke, Massachusetts. After committal sentences and prayer by the minister, Mary's parents took the box containing her ashes and, together, placed it in the grave. Each sprinkled a handful of earth over it. The minister gave a benediction. Those present spontaneously expressed their love to one another and dispersed.

APPENDIX 1:

MUSIC FOR THE FUNERAL SERVICE

Hymns for the Funeral Service

Title	Tune
"A Mighty Fortress"	Ein' feste Burg
"Abide with Me"	Eventide
"All Glory Be to God on High"	Allein Gott in der Höh'
"All People That on Earth Do Dwell"	Old Hundredth
"Be Thou My Vision"	Slane
"Breathe on Me, Breath of God"	Trentham
"Cast Thy Burden on the Lord"	Savannah
"Christ the Lord Is Risen Again"	Christ ist erstanden
"Faith of Our Fathers"	St. Catherine
"For All the Saints"	Sine Nomine
"Glorious Things of Thee Are Spoken"	Austria
"God Moves in a Mysterious Way"	Dundee (French)
"God of Grace and God of Glory"	Cwm Rhondda
"Guide Me, O Thou Great Jehovah"	Cwm Rhondda
"I Know That My Redeemer Lives"	Truro
"I Love Thy Kingdom, Lord"	St. Thomas
"I to the Hills Will Lift My Eyes"	Dundee (French)
"If Thou But Suffer God to Guide Thee"	Neumark (Wer nur den lieben Gott)
"Immortal, Invisible, God Only Wise"	Joanna (St. Denio)

"Jerusalem the Golden"	Ewing
"Joyful, Joyful, We Adore Thee"	Hymn to Joy
"Love Divine, All Loves Excelling"	Beecher
"O God, Our Help in Ages Past"	St. Anne
"O Love That Wilt Not Let Me Go"	St. Margaret
"Of the Father's Love Begotten"	Divinum Mysterium
"Out of the Depths, I Cry to Thee"	Aus Tiefer Noth
"Praise, My Soul, the King of Heaven"	Lauda Anima; Benedic Anima Mea; Regent Square
"Ten Thousand Times Ten Thousand"	Alford
"The Church's One Foundation"	Aurelia
"The King of Love My Shepherd Is"	Dominus Regit Me; St. Columba
"The Lord's My Shepherd"	Belmont; Crimond; Evan; Martyrdom
"The Strife Is O'er"	Palestrina (Victory)
"Who Trusts in God, a Strong Abode"	Bishopgarth

Other hymns appropriate for the funeral service may be used, such as the following:

"All Creatures. . . "
"Canticle of Remembrance"
"Christ the Victorious"
"How Blest Are They Who Trust in Christ"
"If Death My Friend and Me Divide"
"Near to the Heart of God"
"Give Thanks for Life"
"Lord of the Living"
"O Lord of Life, Where'er They Be"

Organ Music

Bossi, C. Adolfo	Elegia
Chesler, Dean	Variations on "Abide With Me"
Foster, Myles B.	"The Good Shepherd"
Marpurg, Friedrich Wilhelm	Chorale Prelude on "Out of the Depths I Cry to Thee"
Pachelbel, Johann	Prelude on "I Cry to Thee, Lord Jesus Christ"
Peters, C. F.	Eighty Chorale Preludes
Powell, Robert	Elegy
Stanford, Charles	Prelude on "The King of Love My Shepherd Is"
Staszeski, Carolos	Prelude on "Belmont"
Vaughan Williams, Ralph	Chorale Prelude on "Rhosymedre"
Young, Gordon/Theodore Presser	Voluntary on "Ein Feste Burg"
Young, Gordon/Theodore Presser	Voluntary on "Olivet"

In addition, slow movements from the six sonatas by Mendelssohn may be used. Hymn settings by Dale Wood and Don Hustad may also be appropriate.

The following collections contain organ pieces appropriate for the funeral service:

A Collection of Funeral Music. Edited by Austin C. Lovelace. Nashville: Abingdon Press, 1962.
The Parish Organist. Edited by H. Fleischer, Erich Gold-

schmidt, Thomas Gieschen, and Willem Mudde. Part X — Music for Funerals and Memorial Services. St. Louis: Concordia Publishing House.

This Is the Victory. Compiled and arranged by G. Winston Cassler. Minneapolis: Augsburg Publishing House, 1969.

Appropriate funeral music may also be found in the following:

Bach, J. S. *Eighteen Large Chorales.* Edited by Riemenschneider. Bryn Mawr, PA: Theodore Presser Co.

———. *Jesu, Joy of Man's Desiring.* New York: H. W. Gray.

———. *The Liturgical Year.* Edited by Riemenschneider. Bryn Mawr, PA: Theodore Presser Co.

Brahms, J. *Eleven Chorale Preludes.* Edited by Biggs. Bryn Mawr, PA: Mercury Music Corp.

Buxtehude, D. *24 Chorale Preludes for Organ.* New York: C. F. Peters Corp.

Davison and Pfatteicher, eds. *Church Organist's Golden Treasury,* Vols. I, II, III. Bryn Mawr, PA: Theodore Presser Co.

Powell, R. *Elegy for Organ.* Nashville: Abingdon Press.

———. *Four Psalm Preludes.* Nashville: Abingdon Press.

Vierne, L. *Twenty-four Pieces in Free Style.* Edited by Durand. Philadelphia: Elkan-Vogel Co.

Willan, Healey. *Six Chorale Preludes, Set 1.* St. Louis: Concordia Publishing House.

For additional suggestions of music appropriate for the funeral service, see the following books:

A Manual for the Funeral. Prepared by the Commission on Worship of the Methodist Church. Nashville: Abingdon Press, 1962.

Music for Church Funerals and Memorial Services, by Frederick A. Snell. Philadelphia: Fortress Press, 1966.

APPENDIX 2:

MODEL SERMONS

Although funeral sermons written by others may be valuable models for the minister who is pressed for time, the temptation to take such a sermon and "stretch" it for a particular funeral occasion should be resisted. Three model sermons are included here to show how others have developed funeral sermons, so that the pastor can become more creative in this task.

The sermon that follows is one that I wrote for the funeral service of a church member who completed suicide. A pseudonym has been used.*

SERMON FOR JOAN JOHNSON

For by grace you have been saved through faith, and this is not your own doing; it is the gift of God.

— Ephesians 2:8

The hymn "Amazing Grace" is said to be the favorite hymn in America. It is so loved because it expresses our feelings as Christians — we are saved by God's amazing grace. The

---

*For additional sermons and resources on suicide, see the bibliography.

unmerited love of God which is a gift of God reaches out to the hearts of every human being.

The words of the first verse speak to us on this occasion as we grieve the death of Joan, who chose to end her own life: "Amazing grace! How sweet the sound that saved a wretch like me! I once was lost, but now am found, was blind, but now I see." We are all saved by the amazing grace of God, not by our works.

As we gather to grieve Joan's untimely death, we ask, Why? Why did she do it? Why didn't we, some one of us, recognize her cries for help and do something to prevent this tragedy? Why did she choose death when she had so much to live for? To know "why" would solve very little. No reason would be enough to set our minds at ease. No reason would restore the joy we have lost in grieving Joan's death.

There is a great mystery about death, and especially a death like Joan's. We cannot explain it. We can only love her in memory, love her family and friends, and commend her to the mercy of our God of amazing grace.

Suicide has been greatly misunderstood. When we examine Scripture we find there are seven suicides mentioned in the Bible. The Bible neither condones nor condemns suicide. Samson, who took his own life in pulling down the pillars of the temple on the Philistines and himself, is numbered as one of the heroes of the faith in the book of Hebrews. Through the ages, individuals have chosen to end their lives, some in self-sacrifice for others as in time of war, others because of intense inner pain, and others for the sake of truth, like Socrates, who drank the hemlock.

This intense inner pain has been called "psychache," a

pain of the psyche. Edwin Schneidman, the father of modern studies of suicide, has helped us better understand this intolerable psychological pain that drives a person to take his or her own life. Most of us at some time or other have felt such inner pain that made us want to escape. Many things in life awaken a longing for death.

Paul Tillich the theologian points out that suicide "actualizes an impulse latent in all life. This is the reason for the presence of suicidal fantasies in most people."* Suicide is a very serious, irreversible act that is triggered by the psychache some feel more intensely than others do. But suicide is not the sin some want to make it. If it were, we all are to be pitied. For deep within each of us, as far away as denial can repress it, is a profound yearning for death. In our moments of despair of life we feel something of what Joan felt when her psychache drove her to end her life.

Suicide is a complex matter. Each person who commits suicide does so for some specific reasons. There are stresses, rejections, failures, and insults that are always present by virtue of living. Some people are able to bear these pains without hurting too much. Others for their own reasons cannot. So for some the thought that cessation of consciousness is the solution to this psychache motivates them to take their own life. The person with an inner pain says to himself or herself, "I won't put up with pain any longer." Death is seen as a means of escape. Death is seen as preferable to living with the intense "storm in the brain" — the psychache. Then comes a lowered

*Tillich, *Systematic Theology,* vol. 3 (Chicago: University of Chicago Press, 1963), p. 57.

threshold for enduring or sustaining the crippling inner pain that drives the person to seek escape by suicide. It is said that there is a twenty minute or so "window of suicide" during which time a person will act to commit suicide. But if they are reached in time, they can be talked through this period or restrained and medicated to prevent them from harming themselves.

The Apostle Paul cried out for release from this body of death: "Wretched man that I am! Who will rescue me from this body of death?" (Rom. 7:24). But this is not the final word. Paul goes on to declare, "Thanks be to God through Jesus Christ our Lord! So then, with my mind I am a slave to the law of God, but with my flesh I am a slave to the law of sin" (v. 25). What allows Paul to give thanks to God through Jesus Christ, even as he longs for escape from this body? Is it not the assurance that nothing separates him from the love of God, the amazing grace that none of us merits, but that is available for all?

So as we grieve the tragic death of Joan, we are not like those who have no hope, for we have a sure and firm hope in God's amazing grace. The Apostle Paul recounts his trials and asks who shall separate us from the love of God in Christ. He answers:

In all these things we are more than conquerors through him who loved us. For I am convinced that neither death, nor life, nor angels, nor rulers, nor things present, nor things to come, nor powers, nor height, nor depth, nor anything else in all creation, will be able to separate us from the love of God in Christ Jesus our Lord. (Rom. 8:37-39)

So we can affirm in the face of this tragic death of Joan Johnson that God's amazing love has overcome death and nothing can separate us from the love of God in Christ Jesus our Lord.

REFLECTIONS ON THE LIFE OF RICHARD T. MEAD*

The facts of Dick Mead's life are well known. They do not need repeating here. Indeed, perhaps nothing at all needs to be said. However, we have come here on this particular day as witnesses to the resurrection of Jesus Christ, because we knew and loved Dick Mead. We have lost a friend, a father, a husband, a teacher, a scholar, a significant and faithful man.

Dick touched all our lives in different ways. No person ever knows another completely, however close the two have been. The reflections of parents on a son's life differ from the reflections of a wife or children. All of our reflections are partial and fragmentary. Their sum total would be less than the whole truth of the person. The very greatness of a person lies in that surpassing wholeness, reserve, and mystery that transcend our knowledge and impressions.

These reflections may capture something of the Dick Mead you knew, or they may not. They are simply the reflections growing out of a friendship that began at Yale Divinity School twenty years ago. They are not inclusive, but they attempt to say something of what I feel and, perchance, something of what you too may feel.

One could not know Dick Mead long without being

*Remarks made by Vanderbilt University Chaplain Beverly Asbury, April 23, 1970. Reprinted by permission.

struck by his thoroughness and care. It would be difficult to believe that he ever did anything carelessly or shoddily. His ability to notice and master detail without ever losing sight of the whole was awesome to lesser mortals. There was never any doubt that his scholarly mind could master both the minutiae and the grander concepts of whatever was before him, whether it was eschatology, baseball, Charlie Brown, or social action.

One could never accuse Dick Mead, however, of being a perfectionist. He never took himself with ultimate seriousness. He had a comic sense and a sense of human comedy. Dick could move from his library carrel to a practical joke with relish and delight, and he could cut through his friends' self-seriousness with redeeming satire, generally historically informed and eruditely expressed.

He knew what to take seriously and what not to. He was capable of a massive indifference to the housekeeping details of life that occupy the Marthas of our world and that make life trivial. He was patient beyond belief. He had goals clearly in sight, but he knew that there was a time for them all, and he waited for the times of their realization in greater hope and patience than most of us can muster.

There was never a doubt that Dick was a "university man." He loved the university, its ways and byways. He never questioned its significance, and he was dedicated to its freedoms and commitments. He served it well. He loved his students and his colleagues equally.

Yet Dick was also a "churchman." He loved the church, its faith and life. The Bible was not only an object of study for him but a deep resource for his own beliefs and actions.

He was not a Christian in any narrow sense. He respected the integrity of other faiths and those who practiced them. He was able to practice Christianity without rejecting others, including those Christians with whom he differed. He loved the church because he had a vision of what she could be and must be in order to be faithful to her Lord. As a churchman, he acted to help create a more just and humane social order for all men.

I suspect that his perspective on his latter days was formed in the crucible of his theological reflections. He confided recently to a friend that he understood his illness as a vicarious role. Since only one in every twenty-five thousand is afflicted with a disease similar to the one that ravaged his body, he could see his burden objectively, statistically, as one that allowed others to live. He accepted his role. He saw death coming. He knew death's presence, as a part of the very structure of life. But he lived life abundantly. He did not allow death to intrude. He treated it as present but inoperative until the time came, hoping in the meantime not to become too great a burden to his family and friends.

And until the time came, he found, as humans do, that what we need most is to be surrounded by love. What finally matters most to us is personal relationships, to love and to be loved. He cherished, accepted, and returned love. Such love is for us a paradigm of God's love, a living sign that Christ is not dead but present among us.

Out of such love for Dick Mead and in celebration of God's love for us, I want to say Hurrah — not flippantly, but gratefully, reverently, loyally:

Hurrah for his dedication, hope, humor,
Hurrah for Dick Mead.

Hurrah for his love and warm humanity.
Hurrah for his courage and endurance.
Hurrah for his dedication, hope, humor, and wit.
Hurrah for Dick Mead, God's good
    and faithful servant.

Glory be to the Father, and to the Son, and to the Holy Ghost; as it was in the beginning, is now, and ever shall be, world without end. Amen.

APPENDIX 3:

SELECTED SCRIPTURE PASSAGES

Old Testament

Psalm 23

The LORD is my shepherd; I shall not want.
He maketh me to lie down in green pastures:
   he leadeth me beside the still waters.
He restoreth my soul:
   he leadeth me in the paths of righteousness
   for his name's sake.
Yea, though I walk through the valley of the shadow of
     death, I will fear no evil:
   for thou art with me;
   thy rod and thy staff they comfort me.
Thou preparest a table before me
   in the presence of mine enemies:
   thou anointest my head with oil,
   my cup runneth over.
Surely goodness and mercy shall follow me all the
     days of my life:
and I shall dwell in the house of the LORD for ever.

(KJV)

The LORD is my shepherd, I shall not want.
   He makes me lie down in green pastures;

he leads me beside still waters;
    he restores my soul.
He leads me in right paths
    for his name's sake.

Even though I walk through the darkest valley,
    I fear no evil
for you are with me;
    your rod and your staff —
    they comfort me.

You prepare a table before me
    in the presence of my enemies;
you anoint my head with oil;
    my cup overflows.
Surely goodness and mercy shall follow me
    all the days of my life,
and I shall dwell in the house of the LORD
    my whole life long.

(NRSV)

Isaiah 40:1-8

Comfort, O comfort my people,
    says your God.
Speak tenderly to Jerusalem,
    and cry to her
    that she has served her term,
    that her penalty is paid,
that she has received from the LORD's hand
    double for all her sins.

A voice cries out:
"In the wilderness prepare the way of the LORD,
    make straight in the desert a highway for our God.
Every valley shall be lifted up,
    and every mountain and hill be made low;
the uneven ground shall become level,
    and the rough places a plain.
Then the glory of the LORD shall be revealed,
    and all people shall see it together,
    for the mouth of the LORD has spoken."

A voice says, "Cry out!"
    And I said, "What shall I cry?"
All people are grass,
    their constancy is like the flower of the field.
The grass withers, the flower fades,
    when the breath of the LORD blows upon it;
    surely the people are grass.
The grass withers, the flower fades;
    but the word of our God will stand forever.

Isaiah 40:28-31

Have you not known? Have you not heard?
The LORD is the everlasting God,
    the Creator of the ends of the earth.
He does not faint or grow weary;
    his understanding is unsearchable.
He gives power to the faint,
    and strengthens the powerless.
Even youths will faint and be weary,
    and the young will fall exhausted;

but those who wait for the LORD shall renew their
    strength,
  they shall mount up with wings like eagles,
they shall run and not be weary,
  they shall walk and not faint.

Isaiah 55:1-3

Ho, everyone who thirsts,
  come to the waters;
and you that have no money,
  come, buy and eat!
Come, buy wine and milk
  without money and without price.
Why do you spend your money for that which is not
    bread,
  and your labor for that which does not satisfy?
Listen carefully to me, and eat what is good,
  and delight yourselves in rich food.
Incline your ear, and come to me;
  listen, so that you may live.
I will make with you an everlasting covenant,
  my steadfast, sure love for David.

Isaiah 55:6-13

Seek the LORD while he may be found,
  call upon him while he is near;
let the wicked forsake their way,
  and the unrighteous their thoughts;
let them return to the LORD, that he may have mercy
    on them,
  and to our God, for he will abundantly pardon.

For my thoughts are not your thoughts,
    nor are your ways my ways, says the LORD.
For as the heavens are higher than the earth,
    so are my ways higher than your ways
and my thoughts than your thoughts.

For as the rain and the snow come down from heaven,
    and do not return there until they have watered the
        earth,
making it bring forth and sprout,
    giving seed to the sower and bread to the eater,
so shall my word be that goes out from my mouth;
    it shall not return to me empty,
but it shall accomplish that which I purpose,
    and succeed in the thing for which I sent it.

For you shall go out in joy,
    and be led back in peace;
the mountains and the hills before you
    shall burst into song,
    and all the trees of the field shall clap their hands.
Instead of the thorn shall come up the cypress;
    instead of the brier shall come up the myrtle;
and it shall be to the LORD for a memorial,
    for an everlasting sign that shall not be cut off.

NEW TESTAMENT

1 Corinthians 15:1-11

Now I would remind you, brothers and sisters, of the good
news that I proclaimed to you, which you in turn received,

in which also you stand, through which also you are being saved, if you hold firmly to the message that I proclaimed to you — unless you have come to believe in vain.

For I handed on to you as of first importance what I in turn had received: that Christ died for our sins in accordance with the scriptures, and that he was buried, and that he was raised on the third day in accordance with the scriptures, and that he appeared to Cephas, then to the twelve. Then he appeared to more than five hundred brothers and sisters at one time, most of whom are still alive, though some have died. Then he appeared to James, then to all the apostles. Last of all, as to one untimely born, he appeared also to me. For I am the least of the apostles, unfit to be called an apostle, because I persecuted the church of God. But by the grace of God I am what I am, and his grace toward me has not been in vain. On the contrary, I worked harder than any of them — though it was not I, but the grace of God that is with me. Whether then it was I or they, so we proclaim and so you have come to believe.

1 Corinthians 15:12-28

Now if Christ is proclaimed as raised from the dead, how can some of you say there is no resurrection of the dead? If there is no resurrection of the dead, then Christ has not been raised; and if Christ has not been raised, then our proclamation has been in vain and your faith has been in vain. We are even found to be misrepresenting God, because we testified of God that he raised Christ — whom he did not raise if it is true that the dead are not raised. For if the dead are not raised, then Christ has not been raised. If Christ has not been raised, your faith is futile and you are still in your sins. Then those also who have died in Christ have perished. If for this life only we have hoped in Christ, we are of all people most to be pitied.

But in fact Christ has been raised from the dead, the first fruits of those who have died. For since death came through a human being, the resurrection of the dead has also come through a human being; for as all die in Adam, so all will be made alive in Christ. But each in his own order: Christ the first fruits, then at his coming those who belong to Christ. Then comes the end, when he hands over the kingdom to God the Father, after he has destroyed every ruler and every authority and power. For he must reign until he has put all his enemies under his feet. The last enemy to be destroyed is death. For "God has put all things in subjection under his feet." But when it says, "All things are put in subjection," it is plain that this does not include the one who put all things in subjection under him. When all things are subjected to him, then the Son himself will also be subjected to the one who put all things in subjection under him, so that God may be all in all.

1 Corinthians 15:35-44

But someone will ask, "How are the dead raised? With what kind of body do they come?" Fool! What you sow does not come to life unless it dies. And as for what you sow, you do not sow the body that is to be, but a bare seed, perhaps of wheat or of some other grain. But God gives it a body as he has chosen, and to each kind of seed its own body. Not all flesh is alike, but there is one flesh for human beings, another for animals, another for birds, and another for fish. There are both heavenly bodies and earthly bodies, but the glory of the heavenly is one thing, and that of the earthly is another. There is one glory of the sun, and another glory of the moon, and another glory of the stars; indeed, star differs from star in glory.

So it is with the resurrection of the dead. What is sown is perishable, what is raised is imperishable. It is sown in dishonor, it is raised in glory. It is sown in weakness, it is raised in power. It is sown a physical body, it is raised a spiritual body. If there is a physical body, there is also a spiritual body.

1 Corinthians 15:45-53

Thus it is written, "The first man, Adam, became a living being"; the last Adam became a life-giving spirit. But it is not the spiritual that is first, but the physical, and then the spiritual. The first man was from the earth, a man of dust; the second man is from heaven. As was the man of dust, so are those who are of the dust; and as is the man of heaven, so are those who are of heaven. Just as we have borne the image of the man of dust, we will also bear the image of the man of heaven.

What I am saying, brothers and sisters, is this: flesh and blood cannot inherit the kingdom of God, nor does the perishable inherit the imperishable. Listen, I will tell you a mystery! We will not all die, but we will all be changed, in a moment, in the twinkling of an eye, at the last trumpet. For the trumpet will sound, and the dead will be raised imperishable, and we will be changed. For this perishable body must put on imperishability, and this mortal body must put on immortality.

1 Corinthians 15:54-58

When this perishable body puts on imperishability, and this mortal body puts on immortality, then the saying that is written will be fulfilled:

"Death has been swallowed up in victory."

"Where, O death, is your victory?

Where, O death, is your sting?"

The sting of death is sin, and the power of sin is the law. But thanks be to God, who gives us the victory through our Lord Jesus Christ.

Therefore, my beloved, be steadfast, immovable, always excelling in the work of the Lord, because you know that in the Lord your labor is not in vain.

Revelation 21:1-7

Then I saw a new heaven and a new earth; for the first heaven and the first earth had passed away, and the sea was no more. And I saw the holy city, the new Jerusalem, coming down out of heaven from God, prepared as a bride adorned for her husband. And I heard a loud voice from the throne saying,

"See, the home of God is among mortals.

He will dwell with them as their God;

they will be his peoples,

and God himself will be with them;

he will wipe every tear from their eyes.

Death will be no more;

mourning and crying and pain will be no more,

for the first things have passed away."

And the one who was seated on the throne said, "See, I am making all things new." Also he said, "Write this, for these words are trustworthy and true." Then he said to me, "It is done! I am the Alpha and the Omega, the beginning and the end. To the thirsty I will give water as a gift from the spring of the water of life. Those who conquer will inherit these things, and I will be their God and they will be my children."

ANNOTATED BIBLIOGRAPHY

DEATH

Anderson, Patricia. *Affairs in Order*. New York: Collier Books, 1991. A complete resource guide to death and dying. Deals with terminal care of the dying, euthanasia and self-deliverance, funeral and disposition of remains, help for the bereaved, and more.

Enright, D. J., ed. *Oxford Book of Death*. New York: Oxford University Press, 1983. A comprehensive book on death useful both for pastors and for study groups dealing with the subject.

Kaiser, Otto, and Eduard Lohse. *Death and Life*. Nashville: Abingdon Press, 1981. An excellent study by two German scholars of the way people of the Bible dealt with death and the meaning of life.

Mills, Liston O., ed. *Perspectives on Death*. Nashville: Abingdon Press, 1969. An excellent symposium on death and the pastoral care of the dying and bereaved. Gives New Testament views of death as well as death in contemporary experience.

Neale, Robert E. *The Art of Dying*. New York: Harper & Row, 1973. Written by a professor of psychiatry and religion, this book offers a series of mental exercises to help individuals face their own death.

A Sourcebook about Christian Death. Chicago: Liturgy Training Publications, 1989.

Thielicke, Helmut. *Living with Death*. Grand Rapids: William B. Eerdmans, 1983. A well-known theologian deals with the meaning of life in the setting of death. Gives an excellent overview of the biblical understanding of death.

FUNERAL PRACTICES

Bowman, Leroy. *The American Funeral*. Westport, CT: Greenwood Press, 1973. Based on five years of research of funeral practices in the United States, this book offers insights on planning a sensible funeral. A landmark in the field.

The United Methodist Book of Worship. Nashville: The United Methodist Publishing House, 1992. Contains slightly revised versions of the liturgies in *The Book of Services* of 1985. Note: The services of *The Book of Worship* were not available from the publisher for inclusion in this edition.

THE FUNERAL SERVICE

Barnes, Marian. *Funerals to Celebrate Life: The Positive Value of Creating an Appropriate Funeral*. East Roseville: Simon and Schuster, 1992.

Book of Common Worship. Prepared by the Theology and Worship Unit of the Presbyterian Church (U.S.A.). Louisville: Westminster/John Knox Press, 1993. Contains the newest Presbyterian liturgies and worship aids.

Dunkle, William F., Jr., and Joseph D. Quillian, Jr., eds. *Companion to the Book of Worship*. Nashville: Abingdon Press, 1970. The chapter "The Funeral" sketches the historical background of the Christian funeral and the rubrics of The United Methodist Church. Shows how rituals reflect doctrines.

Irion, Paul E. *The Funeral: Vestige or Value?* Nashville: Abingdon Press, 1966. Offers a basis for examination, questioning, and criticism of contemporary funeral practices and proposes new designs to conserve real values.

Jackson, Edgar N. *The Christian Funeral*. New York: Channel Press, 1966. Discusses the Christian funeral ceremony and its spiritual values. Contains a variety of funeral meditations.

The Funeral Sermon

Baerwald, Reuben C., ed. *Hope in Grief*. St. Louis: Concordia, 1966. Gives suggestions for making the funeral a service of worship and for developing the funeral sermon, in addition to a collection of sermons and resources.

Chakour, Charles M. *Brief Funeral Meditations*. Nashville: Abingdon Press, 1971. Offers a variety of meditations for particular types of funerals — death of a child, suicide, nonbaptized persons, tragic death, and so on.

Wallis, Charles L., ed. *The Funeral Encyclopedia*. New York: Harper & Brothers, 1953. Contains a variety of funeral sermons, poems, prayers, and guidance for the pastor.

Grief Therapy

Claypool, John. *Tracks of a Fellow Struggler*. Dallas: Word, 1974. A clergyman's personal account of his struggle with grief over the death of his child.

Lewis, C. S. *A Grief Observed*. San Francisco: Harper & Row, 1989. A classic report of the feelings experienced by Lewis over his wife's death. Would be helpful for a grief recovery group or for a bereaved person to read alone.

Nouwen, Henri J. M. *A Letter of Consolation*. San Francisco: Harper & Row, 1982. A letter written to his father six months after the death of Henri Nouwen's mother. A very personal and moving sharing of grief that can aid others who are bereaved.

Reed, Elizabeth Leggett. *Helping Children with the Mystery of Death*. Nashville: Abingdon Press, 1970. Assists teachers and parents in explaining death from a Christian perspective.

Stein, Sara Bonnett. *About Dying: An Open Family Book for Parents and Children Together*. New York: Walker & Co., 1974. Useful in sparking and guiding a family discussion of the taboo subject of death.

Switzer, David K. *The Dynamics of Grief: Its Source, Pain, and Healing*. Nashville: Abingdon Press, 1970. Combines psychological and theological insights on grief and ways to bring about healing. Especially helpful for the pastor.

To Everything There Is a Season: For the Bereaved Christian. Minneapolis: Kairos, n.d. This booklet of Scripture and explanations of the stages of grief is a very helpful resource for the bereaved.

Westburg, Granger E. *Good Grief.* Minneapolis: Fortress/
Augsburg, 1962. A classic study of the stages of grief
by an authority on pastoral care, this little book will
help the pastor and the bereaved become aware of
various stages of grief and learn how to cope. Highly
recommended for use in a grief recovery group.

DEATH OF A SUICIDE

Biddle, Perry H., Jr. *Reflections on Suicide.* Pittsburgh:
Desert Ministries, Inc., 1992. Reviewed by a professor
of pastoral care as a book that "tells what a person needs
to know, feel and do about suicide." Copies are free
from: Desert Ministries, P.O. Box 13235, Pittsburgh, PA
15243.

Clemons, James T. *Sermons on Suicide.* Louisville: West-
minster/John Knox Press, 1989. A collection of sermons on suicide by a variety of preachers, which treat
the subject in a positive, straightforward manner.

Evans, Glen, and Norman L. Farberow. *The Encyclopedia
of Suicide.* New York: Facts on File, 1988. A comprehensive reference on suicide. In an A to Z format, the
book discusses the causes, history, and psychology of
suicide.

Grollman, Earl A. *Suicide.* Boston: Beacon Press, 1988. A
well-known rabbi, in an updated revision of a classic,
discusses suicide and how to comfort the family of a
suicide.

Hewett, John H. *After Suicide.* Louisville: Westmin-
ster/John Knox, 1980. Especially helpful for survivors
of suicide. Tells how to explain suicide to children, and
how to reconcile it with religious beliefs.

ABOUT THE AUTHOR

PERRY H. BIDDLE, JR., is an author and minister-at-large of Middle Tennessee Presbytery, Presbyterian Church (USA). He is a graduate of Davidson College, Davidson, North Carolina, Union Theological Seminary in Virginia, Richmond, Virginia, and Vanderbilt University, Nashville, Tennessee. He also studied at New College, University of Edinburgh, Scotland. He is the author of fifteen books, including *A Marriage Manual, A Hospital Visitation Manual,* and *A Funeral Manual,* three highly acclaimed books on pastoral care.